PIPE FITTINGS

NIPPLES

PIPE LENGTHS UP TO 22 FT.

STRAIGHT COUPLING

REDUCING COUPLING

COUPLING

NUT

CAP

STRAIGHT TEE

REDUCING TEE

STREET TEE

STRAIGHT CROSS

W9-CXQ-623

CROSS

90° ELBOW

90° ELBOW

90° ELBOW · 45° ELBOW · REDUCING ELBOW · 90° STREET ELBOW · 45° STREET ELBOW · 45° Y-BEND

UNION (3 PARTS)

PLUG

BUSHING

CAP

RETURN BEND

REDUCING TEE

REDUCER

90° · 45°
UNION ELBOWS
STREET

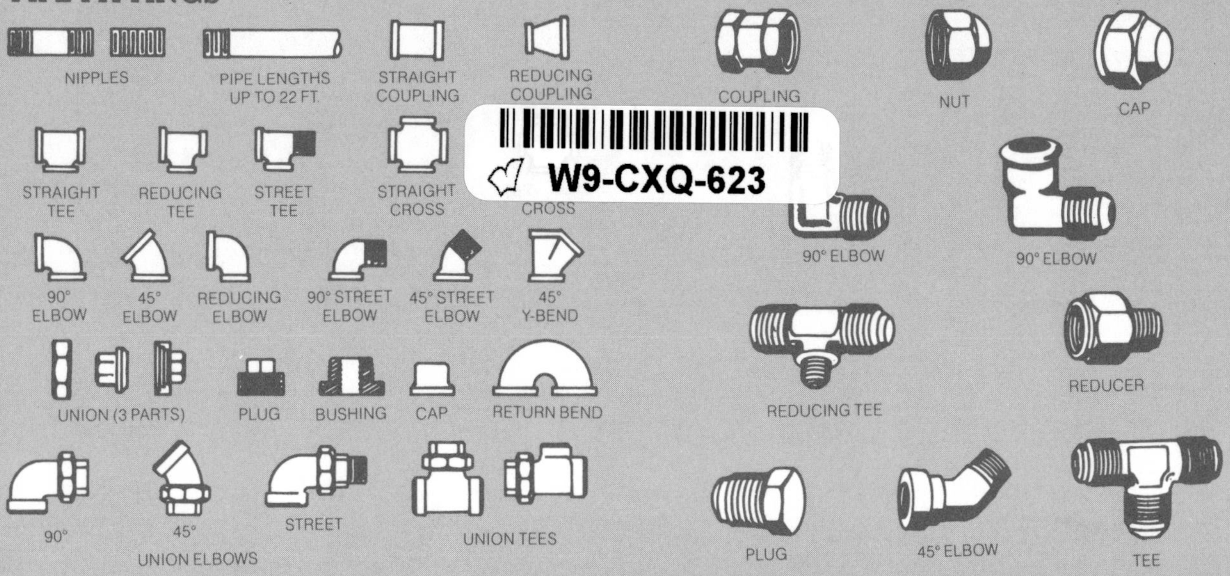

UNION TEES

PLUG · 45° ELBOW · TEE

MEASURES OF CAPACITY

1 cup = 8 fl oz
2 cups = 1 pint
2 pints = 1 quart
4 quarts = 1 gallon
2 gallons = 1 peck
4 pecks = 1 bushel

STANDARD STEEL PIPE ((All Dimensions in inches)					
Nominal Size	Outside Diameter	Inside Diameter	Nominal Size	Outside Diameter	Inside Diameter
⅛	0.405	0.269	1	1.315	1.049
¼	0.540	0.364	1¼	1.660	1.380
⅜	0.675	0.493	1½	1.900	1.610
½	0.840	0.622	2	2.375	2.067
¾	1.050	0.824	2½	2.875	2.469

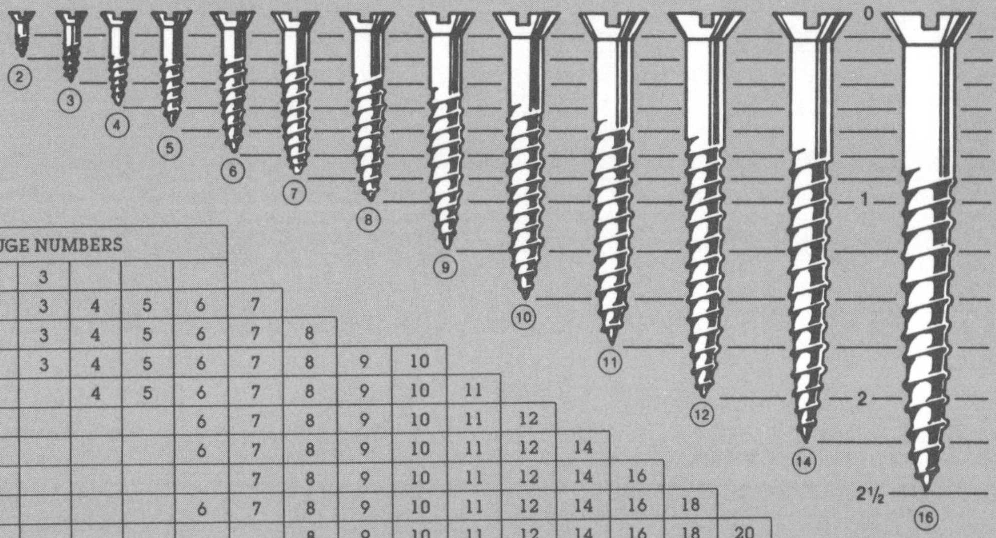

WOOD SCREWS

LENGTH	GAUGE NUMBERS															
¼ INCH	0	1	2	3												
⅜ INCH			2	3	4	5	6	7								
½ INCH			2	3	4	5	6	7	8							
⅝ INCH				3	4	5	6	7	8	9	10					
¾ INCH					4	5	6	7	8	9	10	11				
⅞ INCH							6	7	8	9	10	11	12			
1 INCH							6	7	8	9	10	11	12	14		
1¼ INCH								7	8	9	10	11	12	14	16	
1½ INCH							6	7	8	9	10	11	12	14	16	18
1¾ INCH									8	9	10	11	12	14	16	18	20
2 INCH									8	9	10	11	12	14	16	18	20
2¼ INCH										9	10	11	12	14	16	18	20
2½ INCH													12	14	16	18	20
2¾ INCH														14	16	18	20
3 INCH															16	18	20
3½ INCH																18	20	24
4 INCH																18	20	24

WHEN YOU BUY SCREWS, SPECIFY (1) LENGTH, (2) GAUGE NUMBER, (3) TYPE OF HEAD—FLAT, ROUND, OR OVAL, (4) MATERIAL—STEEL, BRASS, BRONZE, ETC., (5) FINISH—BRIGHT, STEEL BLUED, CADMIUM, NICKEL, OR CHROMIUM PLATED.

Popular Mechanics

do-it-yourself encyclopedia

The complete, illustrated home reference guide from the world's most authoritative source for today's how-to-do-it information.

Volume 18

PHOTOGRAPHY

to

PLAYHOUSES

HEARST DIRECT BOOKS

NEW YORK

Acknowledgements

The Popular Mechanics Encyclopedia is published with the consent and cooperation of POPULAR MECHANICS Magazine.

For POPULAR MECHANICS Magazine:

Editor-in-Chief: *Joe Oldham*
Managing Editor: *Bill Hartford*
Special Features Editor: *Sheldon M. Gallager*
Automotive Editor: *Wade A. Hoyt, SAE*
Home and Shop Editor: *Steve Willson*
Electronics Editor: *Stephen A. Booth*
Boating, Outdoors and Travel Editor: *Timothy H. Cole*
Science Editor: *Dennis Eskow*

Popular Mechanics Encyclopedia

Project Director: *Boyd Griffin*
Manufacturing: *Ron Schoenfeld*
Assistant Editors: *Cynthia W. Lockhart, Peter McCann, Rosanna Petruccio*
Production Coordinator: *Peter McCann*

The staff of Popular Mechanics Encyclopedia is grateful to the following individuals and organizations:

Editor: *C. Edward Cavert*
Editor Emeritus: *Clifford B. Hicks*
Production: *Layla Productions*
Production Director: *Lori Stein*
Book Design: *The Bentwood Studio*
Art Director: *Jos. Trautwein*
Design Consultant: *Suzanne Bennett & Associates*
Illustrations: *AP Graphics, Evelyne Johnson Associates, Popular Mechanics Magazine, Vantage Art.*

ISBN 0-87851-171-7

Library of Congress 85-81760

10 9 8 7 6 5 4

PRINTED IN THE UNITED STATES OF AMERICA

Contributing Writers: James L. Abbott, *Slide copy illuminator*, page 2190; Michael Ray August, *Lighted planters—the way to grow*, page 2253; Paul Bell, *Picnic table that folds flat*, page 2241; Rosario Capotosto, *Blow it up big*, page 2187; Bob Corley, *Wheelbarrow planter*, page 2263; Gary Gerber, *Picnic furniture from chimney blocks*, page 2238; R.S. Hedin, *Seesaw with a new twist*, page 2296; *Stilt-house slide*, page 2298; Charles R. Hentz, *A-frame swing set*, page 2287; John L. Kuik, *Indoor playhouse*, page 2302; Frank LaManna, *Extension flash bracket*, page 2191; Wayne C. Leckey, *Picnic table you can stow away*, page 2246; *Tub planters*, page 2261; James A. Long, *Rustic picture frames from barn siding*, page 2236; Adolph J. Maier, Jr., *Picture framing secrets of a master craftsman*, page 2228; David Miller, *Photography: an introduction*, page 2180; Stephen Menke, *Super sandbox you can build*, page 2285; Al Nunes-Vais, *Floater picture frame*, page 2233; Harvey Shaman, *Add 3-D to your photo display*, page 2219; Charles Smith *Armchair studio for wildlife photos*, page 2193; Gordon Smith, *Display big panoramas from little pictures*, page 2216; Brad Synder, *Playhouse you can build*, page 2299; Robert S. Topper, *Fancy picture frame repair*, page 2234; Al Westerfield and Harry Wicks, *Internal carving: a little-known art*, page 2275; Harry Wicks, *Picture framing techniques*, page 2221.

Cynthia Lockhart, David Miller, Michael Padilla, *Tips for Color Photography.*

Picture Credits: Popular Mechanics Encyclopedia is grateful to the following for permission to reprint their photographs: Photo Researchers, Inc. will henceforth be referred to as P.R., Inc.: Penelope Byham, page 4 color insert (top) and page 5 color insert (bottom left); Kent & Donna Dannen, P.R., Inc., page 2 color insert (bottom left); Mary Ann D'Esopo, P.R., Inc., page 1 color insert; Lowell Georgia, P.R., Inc., page 3 color insert (top and bottom right); Louis Goldman, P.R., Inc., page 8 color insert (top); Don Goode, P.R., Inc., page 6 color insert (bottom); K2 Corp., page 5 color insert (bottom right); LaserColor Laboratories, pages 2216-2217 (top); Herb Levart, P.R., Inc., page 2 color insert (bottom right); George T. Manna, P.R., Inc., page 4 color insert (bottom); Rafael Marcia, P.R., Inc., page 8 color insert (bottom); Olin Ski Co., Inc., page 2183; Carl Purcell, P.R., Inc., page 6 color insert (top); Renee Purse, P.R., Inc., page 3 color insert (bottom left); Albert Squillace, pages 2180, 2181, page 2 color insert (top), page 5 color insert (top left and top right), page 7 color insert (top right); C. Vergara, P.R., Inc., page 7 color insert (bottom right); Larry Voigt, P.R., Inc., page 7 color insert (top left); Daniel Zirinsky, P.R., Inc., page 7 color insert (bottom left).

Contents

Photography: an introduction

■ THERE ARE MANY WAYS OF LOOKING AT THE WORLD, but only two ways of recording it: as you would like it to be or as it is. In either case, one of the best means of recording it is with photography. In its long double life as both a hobby and a profession, photography has been called many things—a science, a craft, an art, a way of recording, a way of seeing, even the art of seeing. Its basic function, however, has not changed. Regardless of what you call it, photography remains a remarkably efficient and accurate method of permanently recording events and objects as they exist in nature.

The scientific system

In theory, the system requires a light source and a camera loaded with a light-sensitive emulsion embedded with silver halide crystals. When the camera's shutter is opened, the light strikes the film, exposing some of the silver crystals. The exposed film is then processed in several chemical baths to bleach out the unexposed silver particles, leaving an image that is fixed permanently by other chemicals.

The human factor

So much for theory. In practice you need a thinking human being to put this scientific system into operation. Equipment needs are basic—even the simplest camera can do the recording job. Today's simple cameras, aided by over 100 years of technological discovery and innovation, are a far cry from their earliest counterparts. They are easier and much more foolproof to use.

But while manufacturers have tried to transform even the most sophisticated professional-type models into point-and-shoot cameras with new push-button technology, they have made little effort to improve the photographer's ability to point at and shoot at the right place and time. With the world so much more readily available to today's photographer, the need to use that equipment properly, to get the most out of it, becomes crucial.

Among the factors that still demand thought and effort from the user are composition, lighting and proper handling of people. Mastering these factors requires more skill than pushing the button on the machine.

COMPOSITION

Composition presents little in the way of problems for the studio photographer who can arrange subjects in any way. It is no problem to the photojournalist who must take the subject matter as it comes. But as an average amateur sharpshooter "in the field," you have your work cut out for you. Recognizing an interesting subject is the first, relatively easy, step. Arranging it to your liking could be troublesome. You can't, for example, move a waterfall to another side of a mountain, but there are ways to "arrange" nature to better suit your needs.

Keep the subject simple

Possibly the most essential rule in composition,

FILM RECORDS AN IMAGE by exposing a silver halide emulsion to a light source, then subjecting the film to chemicals that develop and retain the image.

GOOD PHOTOGRAPHY
requires more than technical skill. A quick eye and good sense of composition are sometimes more important. The photo on the right, taken from an apartment window, uses strong vertical and horizontal lines (compositional elements) and doll-sized workers to make a point about urban crowding .

as in many other aspects, is *keep it simple.* Try to fill the frame of your picture with just the essential subject. Most amateurs don't have the luxury, or the desire, to spend the time and effort to make their own enlargements. Enlarging lets you crop, or isolate, the more important parts of your picture. By concentrating on them, you can eliminate all unwanted elements.

Practice selective cropping in the camera. Using a zoom lens or changing to a longer focal length lens if your camera is equipped to handle them, is the easiest method of in-camera cropping. With simpler, fixed-lens cameras, you have to change your angle of view or shooting distance by moving around and, if possible, closer to your subject.

Keep the background simple

Make the background a part of the composition rather than just another distracting element. With an adjustable lens camera you can choose a larger aperture (and correspondingly faster shutter speed) to lessen depth-of-field. This will throw the background slightly out of focus. If you are able to move your subject around, place it within a large plain area of contrasting color, tone and texture.

Lead eye into the picture

Try not to cut off large shapes at the edges of your picture's frame. This leads the viewer's eye *out of* the picture. That doesn't mean your main subject must always be smack in the middle, but the viewer should always be directed *into,* not out of, the photo. Lines such as the converging parallel tracks of a railroad, furrows in a plowed field or lines of a building should always lead the eye toward the main point of interest.

Fill spaces with foreground objects

If you can't avoid including a large area of minimal interest, it is better to sacrifice the background and keep the essential elements in the foreground. You can sidestep the pitfall of the vast, open area by including an object close to the camera in an upper or lower corner of your frame. Such an object, frequently an overhanging branch, bit of shrubbery or rock, provides a natural framework for a scene as well as helping to fill the void of the large, undetailed area.

Center of visual interest

Another tack you can take, particularly in scenic shots, is to place the main area of interest slightly below the horizontal midpoint of the frame. Another theory suggests dividing the picture area into three equal parts, both horizontally and vertically. Then, place the main and secondary subjects at the various points of intersection of these areas. The main area of interest, therefore, cannot fall in the center of the picture, and

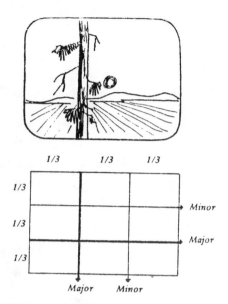

DIVIDE YOUR VIEWFINDER INTO THIRDS both horizontally and vertically. The intersections of the imaginary lines are the primary and secondary focal points of interest.

you have a better chance of eliminating unwanted foreground or background.

Lead eye to essential elements

Since you can't really bend nature to your will, you should look for certain natural shapes and configurations that are photographically pleasing. Perhaps the best known, and most easily recognizable, of these is the classic "S" curve. Whether a complete or partial S, this design always captures, holds and directs the onlooker's eye to the essential areas within the picture's frame. To such shapes as a curving road or stream you should, if possible, add a contrasting element such as a straight line with a well-defined horizon, skyline or building edge.

Use contrast to focus visual interest

Contrasting elements, whether of shapes, tone,

IN SOME CASES, the foreground of a photo is easy to fill. In this case, the photographer waited for a ferryboat to pass by, and maneuvered to get fellow tourists into his picture as well. (New Yorkers will recognize this as an old photo—The World Trade Center now dominates this part of the Manhattan skyline.)

mass or color, are always contributing factors to good composition. Balance of various elements along the main subject line (a row of trees, buildings, etc.) also helps. Symmetry, or balance resulting from objects of equal or similar "weight" and size, is good but not necessary. Placing a round or domed building within a group of sharp, vertically oriented shapes serves to emphasize and locate it as the main point of interest.

Color can define visual interest

Good composition must be applied as much to black-and-white pictures as to color. As a matter of fact, composition is more difficult with black-and-white because tonal differences exist only in brightness and contrast. You have much more leeway with color shooting. You can use not only the color itself, but the variations in tone, saturation, hue, luminosity and "temperature" (red tones represent warmth; blue tones, coolness). In color composition, try to single out a few large, single-colored areas rather than go for the entire spectrum in smaller, multicolored objects. Avoid unpleasant clashing of colors. Generally, cool hues are best for backgrounds, while the warmer tones make for better foregrounds.

Use the shape of the negative

Since most cameras, simple and sophisticated, rely on a rectangular format negative, you can turn this to your advantage. Vertical pictures usually suggest action and movement while horizontal images are better for scenic landscapes, city views and the like. Motion can also be expressed with subjects that "move" or direct the eye along diagonal lines from one upper corner of the frame to the opposite lower corner.

Action shots

As for action shots themselves, good composition begins with an adjustable shutter with a speed of 1/1000 second or faster. If your camera can't oblige, you can still "stop" a moving subject by photographing it head on. This will not only freeze the subject, it might possibly result in a better picture as secondary elements provide the action. For example, the image of a skier making a turn in powder snow may be static but the flying powder, kicked up by the skis—blurred or not—will provide the sense of rapid movement in progress. It could also add drama in the final picture. If you can't shoot the action head on, approach it from the side and pan along with the subject, snapping the shutter as the action reaches a point directly in line with your vantage point.

WHILE FAST SHUTTERS STOP ACTION, you can often gain the effect of action by letting the moving object blur.

Off with their heads!

Avoid cutting off objects along the edges of the frame. Parallax has been responsible for more clipped heads than any revolutionary tribunal in history. Parallax happens in viewfinder cameras because the viewfinder is located at a different place from the lens on the camera and does not "see" from quite the same angle. Camera makers have devised ways of eliminating or compensating for parallax with a frameline in the camera's viewfinder. In some of the more expensive models, the frameline moves as you focus the lens to a closer distance. (Parallax is present primarily at close focusing distances.) In most models, small marks at the corners of the frameline set off the area of the frame to be used at close subject distances. Pay attention to them.

All other rules of good composition should be followed, but they are not quite as rigid. As with any other kind of rules, they are not made just to be broken—but there are exceptions. As with all other creative endeavors, your eye and mind should have a say in the matter, too.

LIGHTING

Lighting is perhaps the most crucial factor in photography. Outdoors, or indoors with available (natural) light, you are at the mercy of the source—the sun. While you can't control its strength, you may be able to control its direction by shifting your position or your subject's posi-

TYPICAL SUNNY-DAY photo, with deep shadow areas on the subjects' faces, is a likely candidate for fill-in flash technique to brighten shadows.

SHOT WAS IMPROVED considerably by simply combining sunlight with flash-fill lighting to give less contrast and add ample detail in shadow areas.

tion. The old sun-over-your-shoulder and directly into-the-eyes-of-your-subject ploy went out with the horse and buggy. Modern cameras and films are capable of handling many tricky and low-level lighting situations. For example, you can use sidelighting for more dramatic shadows and added dimension through modeling.

While sidelighting may produce added interest with inanimate objects, it can wreak havoc with faces since harsh shadows can obliterate crucial facial features. To restore the full face, you can pose your subject in open shade—at the side of a building for example—or hope for overcast or hazy sky. Failing that, you can resort to flash.

Fill-in flash

The technique of using flash to augment outdoor available light, known as *fill-in flash,* has been used by professionals for many years and is just now becoming available to amateurs through specialized but readily obtainable equipment. Automatic electronic flash units are geared to illuminate the subject with just the right amount of light, based on flash-to-subject distance. When used outdoors, they provide the proper lighting for the face while the ambient daylight takes care of exposure for the rest of the scene. Some cameras, notably Polaroid instant models and some 35mm compacts, use systems that calculate the right mixture of flash needed with the ambient light level to produce a properly exposed picture, and then provide the necessary amount of fill-in flash lighting.

Backlighting

Breaking further with tradition, you can pose your subject between you and the sun. The resulting backlighting can produce an effective silhouette, but make sure the subject blocks the sun from your camera. Otherwise the strong sun will fool your camera's exposure system into producing a severely underexposed photo. With an ad-

A SILHOUETTE with backlighting can be effective, but you may have to settle for an overexposed background or underexposed subject.

justable camera you can set exposure for the backlighted subject. The subject will then be rendered properly but at the expense of an overexposed, watered-down background.

Indoor available light

Indoor available light, coming mainly from windows or a skylight, is generally used for sidelighting. If that's not what you're after, you can easily correct it with flash. But straight indoor flash has problems too. A direct blast of light can often result in washed-out faces and harsh shadows. You may be able to eliminate the shadows by moving your subjects away from walls or similar nearby objects. And you may be able to do away with the washout by draping a fold or two of handkerchief over your flash unit's head.

Bounce flash

Such corrective measures become unnecessary if you have a flash unit with a movable head. These units let you aim the head at the ceiling, which gives you a "bounce" flash: the light from the unit hits the ceiling and bounces off, falling lightly over your subject. Since the light must travel a greater distance than when used directly, it is not as powerful when it hits your subject. Result: no distracting shadows in the background, a properly exposed face with virtually no shadows (faintly darker areas under nose and chin are possible, but nowhere as devastating as with direct flash). If your unit is a manual model, you must calculate flash-to-subject distance for

LIGHT COMING FROM A WINDOW can be used indoors for dramatic sidelighting.

the light's entire trip—from the flash to the ceiling to the subject. If it's an automatic unit, proceed normally, since the auto sensor will take care of releasing the correct amount of light as it does with the blast of direct flash.

One major drawback to bounce flash concerns the surface off which you bounce it. If the surface is too strongly colored, it may lead to pictures with an overall color cast matching that of the surface. And extremely high ceilings may be so far away that the light will be dissipated by the

FLASH ON CAMERA creates a photo that is harsh, unflattering. Shadows behind the subjects are distracting. Foreground is overexposed and washed out.

FLASH THAT'S bounced from a photo umbrella gives soft, natural lighting and an even exposure throughout this entire photograph.

GOOD SNAPSHOTS put subjects against a non-distracting background and show them living instead of posing.

time it reaches the subject, giving you, in effect, just another indoor available light shot.

PEOPLE PICTURES

Probably the most difficult subject to manage is people, singly or in groups. Not people in action—people for portraits.

Posing people

Persuading people to pose for you may be a formidable task in its own right, but once they agree, your real troubles begin. Most people become self-conscious and freeze up when placed before the lens. The longer you delay, the more tense they become. So do as much planning as you can before you corral them. Be ready to shoot the moment you get them in focus. Above all, get them to relax. A constant stream of chatter or a good (maybe even a bad) joke may do the trick. But you still have to be ready to snap the shutter at the right instant.

Once you're set up, you might instruct your subjects to close their eyes. Focus and compose carefully and, after enough time for them to settle down, have them open their eyes and catch them after the first blink.

The setting for people

You should give all subjects, cooperative or not, as flattering a surrounding as possible. Keep the background simple—preferably of one solid color complementary to the subject's hair color, clothing, complexion, etc. Use the recommended portrait distance on a fixed lens camera or a lens in the 85mm to 105mm focal length with interchangeable lens models. This eliminates distortion. Turn the subject's head to disguise unflattering features—don't photograph a person with big ears straight on; don't take a profile, or semi-profile, of a subject with a large nose.

Avoid the red-eye special

Flash pictures taken with units close to the camera's lens, as on many simple cameras, can cause "red eye" if the subject is looking directly into the lens. If you can't move the flash off camera, or bounce it, have the subject look off slightly to one side.

Candid pictures

Naturally, candid pictures require different techniques to solve different problems. The main thing is to be ready—always. Keep your lens set at an average distance. If your camera does not have automatic exposure control, keep checking the lighting, adjusting your settings as you move from sun to shade and back again. Candid expressions are much more revealing and usually attractive. Best of all, there's no resistance from the subject.

You can induce candid shots in some instances if you are ready. That means proper exposure settings and prefocusing on your subject. Call out the subject's name, or do something to gain attention, then shoot.

If you are after good people pictures, always be ready to snap that shutter.

CANDID PHOTOGRAPHS are usually better if your subject does not pose but is caught in a natural expression. You have to be ready for these shots.

Blow it up big!

■ WANT TO STARTLE your audience the next time you put on a slide show? Try projecting some extreme close-ups of common household objects and ask your friends to guess what they are. Chances are they'll have a hard time identifying some of the strange-looking results you'll get.

Blown up several hundred times, the eye of a tiny sewing needle comes out so big you could put your head through it. Bristles in a toothbrush take on the appearance of logs the size of telephone poles. Some typical examples of such effects are shown at the bottom of this page.

All you need to produce sensational close-ups like these is a 35-mm single lens reflex camera and the homemade lens adapter shown here. The adapter is essentially a mammoth extension tube. It spaces the regular camera lens about 30 inches away from the film plane, enabling you to make enlargements 10 times actual size. When these are further blown up on a projection screen or in an enlarger, the results are macro-images of tremendous magnification. The adapter is simply a long, square box made of ¼-inch plywood or hardboard and some scraps of ¾-inch solid stock. The camera with its lens removed is mounted at one end of the box and the lens is inserted in the other end. The lens must be turned around and

FAMILIAR OBJECTS look quite different when viewed in extreme close-ups like those at right. Left to right, a lady's nylon stocking, tip of a screw, teeth on a fine machinist's file and toothbrush.

used backward—with its front facing the camera—because a rule of optics requires the elements to be reversed if the distance to the film plane is increased more than eight times the focal length. So size the opening in the end of the box to take the forward barrel of the lens rather than the rear mounting portion.

To join the hole in the camera body to the hole in the other end of the box, you need a short length of adapter tubing. This can be a standard extension tube sold to fit your camera or, for a less expensive dodge, a piece of 1½-inch-diameter drain tailpiece tubing. The latter is a common hardware store plumbing item and has a flange that makes it easy to attach to most SLR cameras. All you need is an accessory screw-in adapter ring to match your camera. Clamp the flange of the tubing between the two parts of the adapter ring and screw the assembly into your camera body. Make the hole in the box a snug fit for whatever tubing you use.

Paint the inside of the box flat black to kill light reflections. A circular light baffle at the box's midpoint also helps to mask off glare. Objects to be photographed are placed in a movable stage made to straddle the base. The stage is slid back and forth to focus the image sharply in the viewfinder instead of focusing the lens itself. Objects too big to fit inside the stage can be stretched across the opening and taped in place.

Exposures must be greatly increased because of the extreme distance between lens and camera. A magnification of 10 times requires an exposure increase of 100. Thus, if a light meter reading indicates an exposure of 1/10th of a second at a given lens opening, the required exposure will be 100 times this or 10 seconds. Work with small lens openings for maximum depth of field and place the setup on a solid surface to avoid movement during the long exposures. Use lenses of at least 50 mm in focal length. An enlarging lens may give even better images than a regular camera lens.

INSIDE OF LENS TUBE is painted flat black to reduce glare that might degrade image clarity. Circular light baffle mounted at center also blocks reflections.

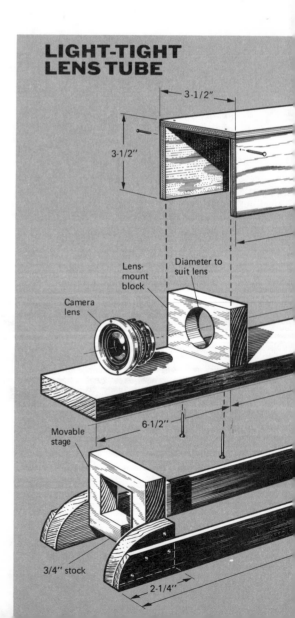

LIGHT-TIGHT LENS TUBE

3-1/2"

3-1/2"

Diameter to suit lens

Lens-mount block

Camera lens

Movable stage

6-1/2"

3/4" stock

2-1/4"

CAMERA BODY can be joined to box with extension tube or short length of plumbing drain clamped between the rings of a standard screw-in lens adapter.

LENS IS MOUNTED in hole at opposite end of box from camera. Remember to reverse lens so front end faces camera.

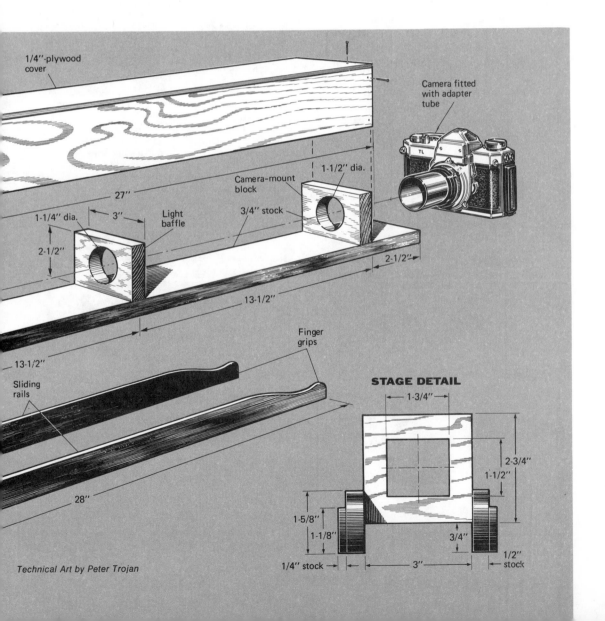

1/4''-plywood cover

Camera fitted with adapter tube

Camera-mount block

1-1/2'' dia.

27''

1-1/4'' dia.

3''

Light baffle

3/4'' stock

2-1/2''

2-1/2''

13-1/2''

13-1/2''

Sliding rails

Finger grips

28''

STAGE DETAIL

1-3/4''

2-3/4''

1-1/2''

1-5/8''

1-1/8''

3/4''

1/4'' stock

3''

1/2'' stock

Technical Art by Peter Trojan

Slide-copy illuminator

■ THIS "SLIDE CONVERTER" lets you shoot with slide film all the time. Then you can convert the results into any other type of film; black-and-white, color negative or duplicate slides. You can make duplicate 35-mm slides and 35-mm copies of 2¼x2¼ (120) slides, and sandwich negatives or positives for unusual effects. But the best of all is the box's cost: less than a dollar.

The box originally held 3½x5-inch photographic printing paper. The 3½x5-inch card that goes just below the lid and the 45° matte-white reflector both can be cut from scraps of poster card stock. A piece of diffusion plastic is available from plastic dealers, among others, for a few cents. You may be able to do without the plastic entirely; but if you try it, make test shots to be sure the opening is evenly illuminated without dark corners.

To use the box, slip your flashgun into the slot,

ALL YOU NEED to copy slides is a camera having close-up gear, an electronic flash and this box. The disassembled view (below) shows the simplicity of construction: just a photo paper box, a white cardboard reflector, a cardboard mask and a piece of plastic diffuser. The flashlight is used to illuminate the slide for focusing. The dimensions shown at left aren't critical, but a smaller box might not fit your flash.

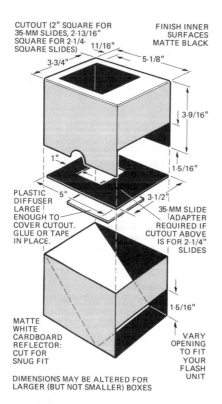

CUTOUT (2" SQUARE FOR 35-MM SLIDES, 2-13/16" SQUARE FOR 2-1/4-SQUARE SLIDES)

FINISH INNER SURFACES MATTE BLACK

11/16"

3-3/4"

5-1/8"

3-9/16"

1"

1-5/16"

PLASTIC DIFFUSER LARGE ENOUGH TO COVER CUTOUT. GLUE OR TAPE IN PLACE.

5"

3-1/2"

35-MM SLIDE ADAPTER REQUIRED IF CUTOUT ABOVE IS FOR 2-1/4" SLIDES

MATTE WHITE CARDBOARD REFLECTOR: CUT FOR SNUG FIT

1-5/16"

VARY OPENING TO FIT YOUR FLASH UNIT

DIMENSIONS MAY BE ALTERED FOR LARGER (BUT NOT SMALLER) BOXES

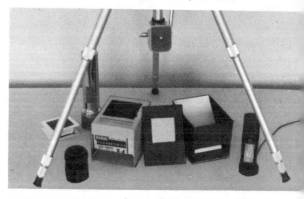

mount your camera above the box with extension tubes or bellows to let you get close enough, and drop the slide you want to copy into one of the holes on top of the box. The 2x2-inch lower opening will block off part of a 2¼-square slide—but not as much as you think: just 1/16 inch from each edge of the visible image area. If you use only 2¼-squares, you can do without the inner adapter plate. (If you don't make 2¼-square slides, you can cut a 2x2-inch hole in the box top, and do without the inner adapter.)

Extension flash bracket you can build

■ THE FLASH BRACKET shown here holds the strobe high above the camera and swings to keep it over the lens whether the camera is vertical or horizontal. The lightweight bracket design is easily customized to suit your needs. The center post adjusts to raise the light even higher. Since the post is removable, the flash can be switched to a similar bracket on another camera without removing the whole mount.

A bracket like this one will help you avoid a red-eye effect in slides and prints where the pupils of the eye seem to be red dots. The bracket prevents the bounce-back reflections causing the problem.

Our bracket also prevents harsh shadows caused by turning the camera vertically and having your strobe off to the side.

Begin by measuring how high above the camera you wish the flash to be. Allow about 8 inches above the lens plus enough more to let the lower end of the flash arm extend 2½ inches below the base of the camera. Mark this length on the square aluminum tubing. Use a hacksaw to cut the tubing.

Measure 1½ inches from one end of the tubing and position the hinge pin there. Mark locations of the screw holes and remove the hinge.

Cut a 4-in length of the ¾-inch wood stock and insert it into the aluminum tubing. Using a ³⁄₃₂-inch bit, drill the holes marked on the aluminum so the bit slightly penetrates the wood. Trim the ends of the hinge leaves to allow clearance for the elbow catches. Attach the hinge to the aluminum, making sure the screws are seated in the wood. The screws will form threads in the soft aluminum, and thread into the wood for added strength.

Cut a second piece of aluminum tubing approximately 3 inches long. Cut a ⅜x⅜-inch notch into one end to provide clearance for the hinge pin. Fit the hinge pin in this notch and mark lo-

DUAL-PURPOSE strobe bracket helps eliminate "red-eye" effect and provides more pleasing, shadowless lighting. Its hinged arm flips to best position no matter which way you hold camera.

cations of the remaining screw holes. Cut a 2¾-inch length of the wood stock and insert it into the tubing. Drill holes and attach the hinge, driving screws all the way into the wood.

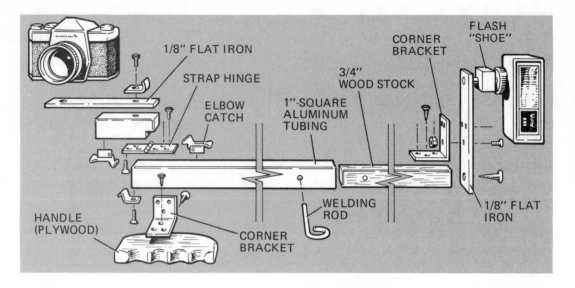

Cut a 6-inch piece of 1/8x1-inch flat steel-bar stock and place it on top of the 3-inch length of tubing as shown. Drill a 3/32-inch hole about 3/8 to 1/2 inch from the end nearest the flash arm. This hole should go through the steel and aluminum into the wood. Enlarge the hole in the steel using a 1/8-inch bit. Attach the steel to the aluminum tubing.

Test-position the striker and elbow catch so they will hold the flash arm properly in the up position. Mark the hole in the striker plate on the steel bar. Drill a hole through to the wood with a 3/32-inch bit, then enlarge the hole in the steel to 1/8 inch. Use a screw to hold the striker plate in place. Place the catch, drill the necessary 3/32-inch holes and attach with the screws provided. Adjust with washers if needed. File all edges smooth. Carefully drill a 1/4-inch hole in the steel bar about 2 inches in from the opposite end. This is for attaching the flash bracket to your camera using a 1/4-20 thumbscrew in the tripod socket. Attach the second striker and catch in the same way as the first.

Insert the remainder of the 3/4-inch wood stock into the top of the vertical flash arm and cut it off so it protrudes about 1½ inches above the tubing. To this protruding end, attach the 1½-inch corner bracket as shown, using wood screws. Position a second 6-inch length of 1/8x1-inch bar stock over this bracket, allowing a 3/4-inch overlap so that the bar can be screwed to the top of the flash post.

Drill out all of the necessary holes and assemble the bar and bracket to the post. Drill a 1/4-inch hole in the opposite end of the bar to line up with the mounting hole in the lower bar.

With the square stock in the tubing, drill a 1/8-inch hole as shown. Raise the post 1 inch and repeat. Continue at one-inch intervals as far as you wish. These holes allow the height of the flash arm to be adjusted.

Next, insert a piece of welding rod into the desired hole and kink it slightly to keep it from falling out. (A rubber band will also help to hold it in place.)

Mount a flash shoe on the upper steel bar using a 1/4-20 machine screw. For further flash adjustment, especially important in closeups, you may wish to add a ball-and-socket swivel between the shoe and your camera. These are available to fit a standard flash shoe and will accept the foot on your strobe.

Shape the 3/4-inch plywood with a coping saw to make a comfortable grip for your hand. Sand the edges smooth. Fasten the grip to the side of the vertical flash post using a right-angle bracket or a length of 1/8-inch bar stock bent to an angle.

Finish by gluing a rubber strip to the base plate and spraying the unit black. Attach your camera to the bracket, slip your flash in the shoe, and connect the strobe to the camera with an accessory coil cord. You should be cautious about using this bracket with wide-angle lenses as the angle of the flash may not be sufficient to cover the entire angle of the lens.

MATERIALS LIST—FLASH BRACKET	
No.	**Size and description**
1	2" strap hinge
2	Elbow catches
1	1/2"-sq. aluminum tubing
1	1½" corner bracket
1	3/4 × 3/4 × 24" pine or hardwood
1	3/4 × 5 × 7" plywood
1	6 × 1" rubber strip

Misc.: Roundhead No. 6 3/4" wood screws, 1/8 × 3/4" round-head bolts with lock washers and nuts, flash shoe threaded 1/4"-20, short piece of welding rod.

Armchair studio for wildlife photos

SETUP IS SIMPLE: Log with holes to hold seed acts as a feeder to attract birds, doubles as a natural background. One-way mirror hides camera from birds.

■ MUCH AS YOU MAY ADMIRE nature photographers who stalk birds through chilly woods for days, you may prefer to get bird shots like this without leaving your armchair—and you can.

The secret is a windowsill bird feeder, with a piece of one-way mirror backing up the window's glass. Invisible to the birds, you can just sit back and click your camera. It takes some patience— but not the field photographer's dedication—and no discomfort.

You can have the mirror cut to any size you wish, according to your budget. A good size to start with is a 5 by 7-in. mirror. If friends and family members start nosing the glass to watch the birds outside, you can switch to a 12 by 30-in. size. For safety and convenience, frame the glass. You can use a rabbeted wood frame, or you can tape the glass in a frame of fiberboard.

The mirror cuts down the light reaching your camera, but you can still shoot, hand-held or on a tripod, with high-speed film. Using these films means you'll get natural-action blurs when the birds move. But the setup can result in cluttered backgrounds, and the faster film has more grain.

You can use slow black-and-white film or color film for wire-sharp, low-grain photos of unblurred action if you mount one or two electronic flash units on the windowsill as illustrated, and run extension sync cords to the camera. (Holes in the window sash or sill are optional.) Since this makes the birds much brighter than the background, there's no more background clutter.

The feeder is a log with holes drilled into it to hold seeds. It also makes a natural-looking setting. When you use flash, attach lights to a 2x4 base and adjust them before putting the light assembly outside, so you disturb the birds as little as possible.

Don't count on good shots your first day—it takes several days from the time you first start putting seed out until your birds find out where it is. Even when you're not taking photographs, the endless antics of the birds entertain family and guests. And if you're looking for a gift for someone who must spend a lot of time indoors, the bird log and mirror, installed, make a fine one, whether they are used with a camera or not.

BLACK AND WHITE print of color photo shows how easy it is to get a "deep-woods" picture from easy chair.

Hints for photographers

A PICTURE FRAME makes a low-cost photo proofer: The quickest, easiest way to evaluate your shooting is by contact-printing a proof sheet for each roll you shoot. But commercial proofing easels cost over $10, and the cheapest, simplest alternative—a sheet of plate glass—is likely to collect fingerprints, or slip out of your hands and shatter on the floor.

But you can build your own proofer. Materials are just a 9x12 picture frame with glass, a piece of ½-inch plywood cut to the frame's outside dimensions, a 12-inch square of indoor-outdoor carpet, plus hinges and tack bumpers.

To start, remove the small nails or wires which hold the glass in the frame and take out the glass. Then line the frame's inside rim with glue, replace the glass and weight it with a heavy book till dry.

While that's drying, paint the bottom and edges of the plywood (but not the top), and put a tack bumper on each corner of the bottom. When the paint dries, place the frame on the base and secure the hinges. Then glue the carpet square—face down and foam backing up—to the plywood base. Trim away the excess. A bulletin-board pushpin in the frame side opposite the hinge makes a good lifting handle.

SPONGE HOLDS DARKROOM THERMOMETERS: Need a safe, convenient place to hold your darkroom thermometers? Cut holes in a large plastic sponge, using a sharpened piece of quarter-inch copper tubing as a cutter. The holes in the low-cost "rack" will hold the thermometers and stirring rods conveniently—and you can still use the sponge for wiping up darkroom spills.

DATA SHEET A HANDY FILM REMINDER: You won't forget what's in your camera if you fold the film's data sheet and tuck it into your camera case with the film's name showing. What's more, that leaves the data sheet right there when you want it for checking exposure, filter factors or anything else you may suddenly want to know about before you push the button.

HERE'S AN EASY WAY TO FILE your negatives where you can find them again. Glue No. 6-¾ (3-⅝ x 6½ in.) envelopes to loose-leaf notebook pages, four or five to each side of the paper, overlapping them so that only the flaps are visible. Identify the negatives in each envelope by writing the subject name or film number on the flaps. Then file in a ring binder. If you have a lot of negatives, you can restrict each page to negative subjects starting with the same letter, then file them between alphabetical index separator pages.

A SIMPLE EFFECTIVE VIGNETTER may be made by cutting a toilet paper roll in two, painting its interior flat black, and carefully slipping it over the lens (or into a filter adapter ring) of a reflex camera. For a twin-lens reflex, use two identical vignetters. To vary the effect, change tube lengths: a longer tube will vignette more, a shorter one will vignette less.

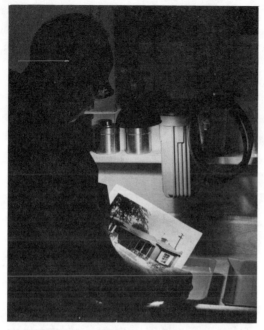

AN INSPECTION LIGHT above the fixing tray is convenient; here's how to switch it on easily.

NUDGE THE BAR (arrow) with your knee and the light goes on. Release it and the light goes off.

KNEE SWITCH for print-inspection light: The best way to judge the quality of your prints is with a white light over the fixer tray. But turning that light on and off as needed can be both a nuisance and a potential shock hazard. This knee switch can take care of both of those problems.

All parts are standard hardware or electrical items, except for the wood pressure bar. Dimensions of the bar are not critical, but its ¼-inch holes

should be counterbored ¾ inch to receive the washers on the switch actuator (4, on photo, facing page) and spring assembly (3). Locate the bar at knee level on your sink or counter front, near the fixer tray. The light may be turned on safely once the print has been in the fixer 20 seconds.

Parts are shown in approximately their assembled relationship. The switch (6) is a normally open type, mounted in a standard receptacle box, with

WALL-HANG YOUR EASEL: Two pieces of molding, one turn-button and four mounting screws can solve the problem of storing enlarging easels out of the way when not in use.

The easel actually rests behind the lip on the upper edge of the lower molding; the turn-button on the upper molding (which has no lip) holds it

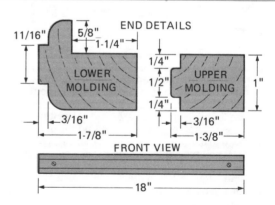

securely. Exact dimensions should be determined for your easel—the ones indicated here are for the 16x20 easel shown. With an easel of this size and weight, the moldings should be attached to your wall's studs; with smaller easels, the moldings can be mounted to a ¼-inch-plywood back and attached with two screws to a single stud.

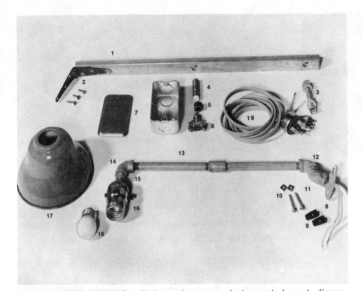

List of parts for inspection light

1. Pressure bar, 13/16 x 1¼ x 20" hardwood.
2. 3" strap hinge and screws.
3. Guide bolt, compression-spring nuts and washers.
4. ½ x 2" metal rod with rubber bumper at switch end.
5. ½ x ¾" bronze bearing.
6. Momentary switch N-O (normally open).
7. Receptacle box and cover.
8. ¼" pipe waste nut and thread nipple.
9. Solderless connectors.
10. 3/16 x 1½" mounting bolts plus nuts.
11. ¼" elbow.
12. ¼" elbow and thread nipple.
13. ¼ x 12" pipe.
14. ¼" elbow.
15. Reducer ¼ to ⅛" pipe, plus ⅛" pipe thread nipple.
16. Standard switch socket.
17. Bell-type reflector.
18. 7½-w. frosted lamp.
19. Three-wire cord with grounding plug and crimp connectors.

EXACT PARTS NEEDED will depend on your darkroom's layout, dimensions and other requirements. But as the picture shows, all parts can be made from standard switches and electrical hardware, stock pipe and pipe fittings, wood, metal rod, and other normal odds and ends from your shop. Even the guide bolt and compression-spring assembly (3) is made up from common, easy-to-find hardware.

washers holding it in place in one of the box's knockouts. Locate this box under the sink, where it won't get splashed, and make sure it's properly grounded to the third wire of the three-wire plug, or directly to a waterpipe.

Where you mount the light fixture will depend on your darkroom setup. A light can be mounted with pipe fittings to the side of a cabinet, so it can be swung out of the way when not in use. The wire runs through the pipe, then inside the wall to the box under the sink. Make sure everything is solid and protected from moisture, and ground the light assembly either to the third wire or a water pipe. It's wise to use a socket with a switch you can turn off when loading film, so an accidental nudge of the knee switch won't cause a darkroom disaster.

CHEAP ENLARGER DUST COVER: Keeping your enlarger dust-free can save you hours of print-spotting. But enlarger dust covers are expensive and not readily available as few dealers stock them. Plastic trash bags can do the same job for just a few cents. Here, a 30-gallon trash bag covers a big Beseler 23C. Smaller bags can store chemical trays and other darkroom items.

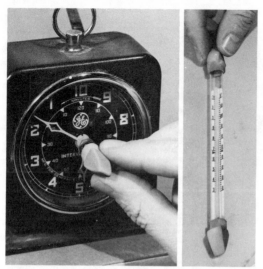

ERASERS CUT DARKROOM ERRORS: The rubber erasers that slip onto pencils can slip helpfully into your darkroom, too. They can give you a better grip on the knobs of some photo timers (above, left), while keeping the timer's metal from contamination by any photo chemicals on your hands. And erasers over the ends of glass darkroom thermometers (above, right) help protect them from breakage, without interfering with temperature measurement.

HOW TO RESTRAIN A CABLE RELEASE: Cable releases have a way of swinging in front of your lens just as you shoot, but they may bind if you wrap them around the camera to prevent this. An easy way to keep your cable release where you want it is to restrain it with a plastic cable tie, or with one of the plastic ties often supplied with plastic trash bags. On some cameras, the tie will pass through the camera's neckstrap slot or "D" ring; on most others, it can be pierced to fit over the camera's strap lug or some other projection.

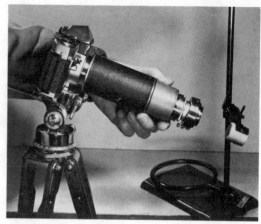

SHOOTING COIN (see below); note reversed lens.

INTERCHANGEABLE inside tubes add versatility; here, to hold one lens normally and another reversed.

SHARP CLOSE-UP made with setup on opposite page; this token has been enlarged four or five diameters.

REVERSIBLE-LENS FOCUSING TUBE

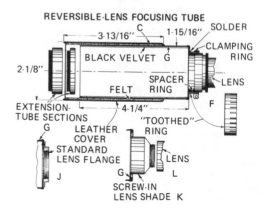

INSTEAD OF A BELLOWS close-up attachment for a single-lens reflex, you can build an adjustable focusing tube—from junk parts. Basically, it's just two tubes, one sliding within the other (see diagram at left). Make the outer tube (C in the diagram, also in photo above) from a small frozen-juice can, with one end removed. The inner tube (G in diagram and photo) could be another can, if you have one that fits, or a cardboard tube with a metal end cap.

Cement a lining of dark felt inside the outer tube, to provide a light-tight seal and a cushion for the inner tube to slide in without play. Cut a carefully centered hole in the back end of the outer tube, just large enough to clear your lens mount; then screw two short, extension-tube sections through the hole (see diagram) so you can mount the completed focusing tube to your camera.

Line the inner, sliding tube with black velvet, or other nonreflecting material. Make another carefully centered hole in this tube's end cap, for a fitting to hold your lens. This could be a standard lens flange (J in the diagram); it would either bolt on or screw on with a retaining ring. Reversing adapters, also available for many lenses, allow you to reverse the lens end-for-end for a little added sharpness in extreme close-ups; if you can't find one, you could make a clamping attachment like that shown as ''F'' in the diagram. Cut a ring from brass tubing, saw slots to form a series of clamping fingers, line it with plastic electrical tape and compress with a screw-tightened ring or hose clamp, to hold it on the lens barrel. This ring can be soldered or welded to the end cap. Or you can fasten a lens shade to the tube, and screw on the lens, reversed.

FOCUS-TUBE PARTS: Extension tubes (A) hold juice-can outer tube (C) to camera; lining of felt (H) inside C seals and cushions slide of inner cardboard tube (G). Lenses (D, L) can be fastened with lens flanges (not shown), with reversed lens-hood (K) to fit lens (L), or with toothed ring (F) made from brass pipe (B) and clamped to lens with clamping ring (E). For details, see diagram on page at left and text.

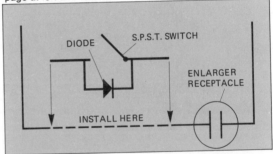

DIODE DIMS ENLARGER: Printing ''thin'' negatives requires either stopping down your enlarger lens to f/22 (not its sharpest aperture), using exposure times too short to allow dodging and burning-in, or both.

This simple intensity switch can help by allowing you to cut your enlarger's light output in half whenever you need to. It's simply an s.p.s.t. toggle switch placed in parallel with a silicon diode and wired into your timer's enlarger socket. With the switch open, the diode allows only half of each a.c. cycle to power the lamp. Closing the switch restores normal operation. The diode should have a rating of at least 2 amps. at 400 PIV. Polarity is unimportant.

If there's no room in your timer for the switch, you can mount the switch, diode, and a duplicate receptacle in a minibox. Remember to connect the box between the timer and the enlarger, not between the timer and the a.c. line.

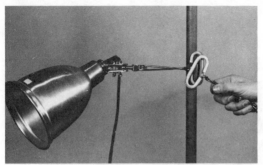

DOUBLED CLAMP IS TWICE AS STEADY: If your clamp-on photo lamps slip because their clamps are loosening, you can hold them in place by placing another spring clamp over the first one.

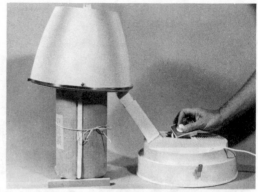

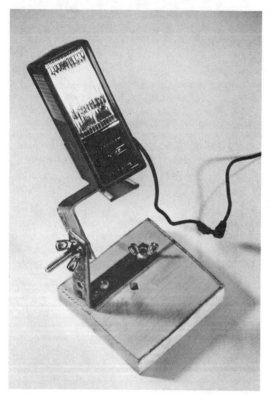

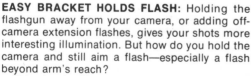

EASY BRACKET HOLDS FLASH: Holding the flashgun away from your camera, or adding off-camera extension flashes, gives your shots more interesting illumination. But how do you hold the camera and still aim a flash—especially a flash beyond arm's reach?

This simple stand can do it for you. It can be made in minutes from a small square of scrap ¾-inch lumber, plus a pair of standard 3-inch angle irons and a pair of ¼-inch bolts with wingnuts.

The mounting shoe for the flash is cut from a tin can, then formed with pliers and its sharp edges filed. A ¼-20 nut epoxied into a hole in the wood base (or a ¼-20 T-nut) also permits tripod mounting when required.

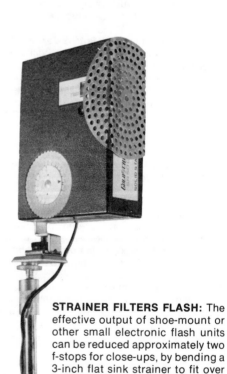

STRAINER FILTERS FLASH: The effective output of shoe-mount or other small electronic flash units can be reduced approximately two f-stops for close-ups, by bending a 3-inch flat sink strainer to fit over the flash head. Spring tension will hold it in place. Since strainers vary, make some tests first.

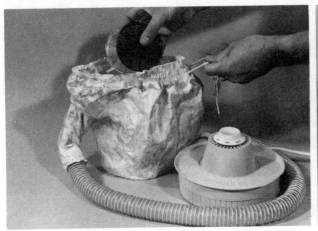 

HAIR DRYERS, FANS EASE DRYING: Hair dryers have a lot of uses in the darkroom. The hard-hood type is an excellent device for quickly drying prints in a blotter roll; just be sure you prop up the roll as shown so air can circulate beneath it. With a coathanger wire beneath the hood, it also dries 4x5-inch sheet film. For roll film, place the dryer at the edge of the counter, and let the film hang down. If your film curls, use a lower heat. A soft-hooded dryer dries plastic developing tank reels quickly after one reel's developed, so you can load the next roll of film without its sticking. And the modern square type of household fan makes an ideal dryer for reels, print tongs and other paraphernalia. Just make hanger clips from light wire to hold everything to the grille, and place a damp towel over the back of the fan to filter out dust.

DARKEN YOUR DOOR with weatherstripping. Close your darkroom door and stand there long enough to let your eyes accustom themselves to the darkness. You'll probably find it's not that dark, after all. Few doors make really light-tight fits into their frames.

But there's an easy way to seal your darkroom door and make it really light-tight: Use automotive weatherstripping. Because the adhesive that comes on the back of the stripping is messy and doesn't hold well if moved, first lay down a strip of double-sided masking tape which is clean, efficient and moveable. Then run the black automotive stripping on top of this. The tape can be pulled off later, if need be, without marring the finish of the wood.

ENLARGING LENS SLIPS under shelf: If you use more than one size of film, you'll need more than one enlarging lens—and a place to store whichever lens isn't in use. Two slotted lumber scraps under a darkroom shelf will hold the lens handily, complete with lens board. The shelf will help keep dust off the lens, but if you have lens caps, use them.

PLASTIC "FERROTYPE" FOR COLOR PRINTS: Do your ferrotyped color prints have measles? Those stains are due to pits and scratches in the ferrotype plate's surface. For foolproof color ferrotyping, cut a new plate from clear plastic "window glass," sold by builders' supply stores. In hot or dry weather, cover the prints with old newspapers once they're on the plate, so drying will be slow and even.

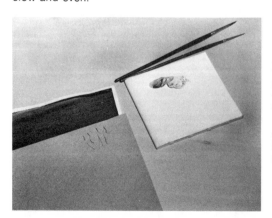

GUITAR STRAP EASES CAMERA LOAD: Ever need relief after carrying a camera and gadget bag around through a full day's shooting? Most weekend photographers overload themselves with gear, then suffer aches and pains from muscles they don't use during the week unless they're postmen. A touch of arthritis made one shutterbug look for something easier on his shoulders than the narrow straps and pads now sold for photo use. He found the answer in colorful, extra-wide guitar straps—two-inch straps for his camera and three-inch for his gadget bag—distributing the equipment's weight over the largest possible body area, and relieving muscular strain. The straps are strong enough to carry your equipment safely, and they can cost less than a good strap pad.

To mount them, cut your camera and gadget-bag straps down to three-inch stubs, and have a shoe-repair shop stub-rivet the stubs to the guitar strap's leather tab end.

AIDS TO EASIER PRINT-SPOTTING: Print-spotting gets a lot less tedious if you work on only one section of a print at a time, blocking off the rest of the area with a sheet of white or yellow construction paper. This paper also doubles as a blotter for removing excess spotting fluid from your brush. And a plain, white, 4-inch-square tile from the hardware store is great for mixing the spotting dyes.

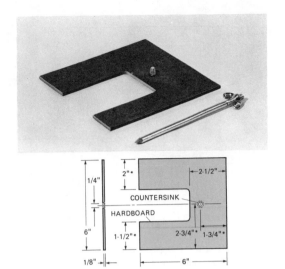

*OR POSITION TO MATCH YOUR CAMERA

CLOSE-UPS of low-lying flowers and the like—or low-angle shots of larger objects—are easy with the flatpod (shown in use above) and the spikepod (upper photo at right). Flatpod construction (lower photo at right) is simple; the only materials are a ¼-20 screw and a piece of hardboard; unit works indoors or out. The spikepod is for use in soft ground.

THIS INDOOR-OUTDOOR CAMERAPOD provides low-level close-ups, which normally aren't easy. Tripods which can hold a camera close to the ground often require accessories. And why tote two feet of tripod to hold a camera at a two-inch elevation? These solutions—the flatpod and spikepod—fit in your pocket.

The flatpod is made from a 6x6-inch scrap of hardboard. Cut a slot as shown for lens clearance, drill and countersink ¼-inch hole for a ¼-20 x ⅜-inch flathead bolt, and you have a low-level stand that will hold your camera and most macro lenses steady on any reasonably level surface. The lens clearance slot and tripod screw positions shown are for a Nikon; you may have to adjust them to fit other cameras.

The spikepod is even simpler: just hacksaw off the head of a long ¼-20 carriage bolt and file the cut end to a point. Add a wingnut to tighten the spike to the camera. To use, just jam the spike into the ground. You can use three, four or six-inch bolts.

FILM HOLDER ENDS FUMBLING: Tired of groping for film in the bottom of your gadget bag? This easy-to-make film holder will end that. All you need is a 1x5-inch strip of hardboard, three 4-40 screws with nuts and lockwashers and six extra film cans. Drill a ⅛-inch hole in the bottom of each film can, and in the hardboard strip at the middle and ½ inch from each end. Attach two cans opposite each other at each hole. The new plastic film cans can be spaced closer together, but washers should then be used. If you like, you can drill an additional hole between two cans for a string to hold the strip on your belt or shoulder strap.

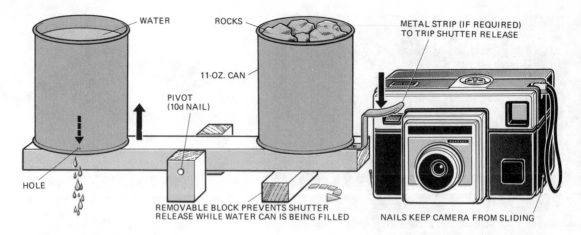

WATER-DRIP SELF-TIMER: Simple cameras don't have self-timers—and often lack cable-release sockets for accessory timer units. But here's a timer you can make. On one end of a 15-inch seesaw stick, mount a soup can filled with enough weight in pebbles to trip your camera's shutter. The other can holds a greater weight of water. A small hole in that can lets the water run out slowly until the balance shifts and the rocks trip the shutter. A block of wood under the can of stones keeps the shutter from tripping accidentally until you remove it.

You can calibrate the water can for different delays, but 10 seconds seems best; too much more time, and the subjects get restless and change expressions—too little time, and you can't get into place before the shutter snaps. A bonus: most subjects are too fascinated by this weird gizmo to think about getting stiff and self-conscious.

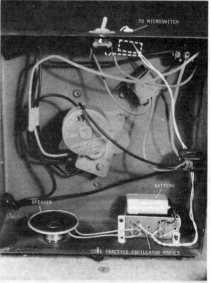

BEEPER IMPROVES LAB TIMER: You can use your timer for both printing and film developing. Since you can't always look up to see when you should agitate the film or paper, the added a "beeper" to sound off once per minute while the timer hands are moving. Parts used were a lever-type microswitch, mounted to contact the second hand as it passes the 60-second mark, a small speaker, and a hobbyist's code oscillator module with its battery taped on; The oscillator is mounted inside the timer case with aluminum brackets, and the speaker is epoxied directly to the case. (There is adequate sound without baffle holes.) The microswitch is mounted on a small wood spacer, so it won't interfere with the minute hand's operation.

MAKE A BROOMSTICK UNIPOD: Add one more leg to the two you have already, and you're a tripod. That's the unipod principle. And while you and the unipod together aren't quite as shake-free as a true tripod, the unipod's much easier to carry.

A homemade version doesn't telescope like the commercial ones, but it's a lot cheaper, and at least as light and sturdy. All you need is a length of 7/8-inch dowel, a 7/8-inch cane tip, a bicycle handlegrip, and a camera-case retaining screw (available from photo dealers).

To put it all together, tape the retaining screw to one end of the dowel securely; then coat that end with glue and push the handlegrip down tightly over that end till the screw threads extend through the grip's end hole (most grips have one, but if yours doesn't, it's easy to punch or cut). Seat the cane tip on the dowel's other end, and you're done.

Length is up to you: A dowel long enough to raise your camera's finder to your eye level is steadiest, but most awkward to carry. This one is 36 inches high so it will double as a walking stick, and you squat or sit to use it. A tripod hanger ring helps keep the screw threads clean when not in use, and lets you attach a rawhide thong as a wrist strap. Another useful option is a golfshoe spike in the bottom, covered by the cane tip when it's not in use.

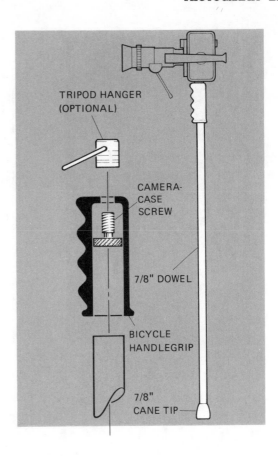

TRIPOD HANGER (OPTIONAL)

CAMERA-CASE SCREW

7/8" DOWEL

BICYCLE HANDLEGRIP

7/8" CANE TIP

REMOVING CAMERA-CASE FROM TRIPOD: If you keep your camera in its case when it's on a tripod, you've probably found that turning the tripod screw often just turns the case screw around and around, loosening the camera, but leaving the case stuck to the tripod. And you can seldom get tools in between the case and the tripod head to grip and hold the screw.

A preventive is to drill, beforehand, one or more holes in the case screw's knurled edge, to take a nail that can act as a gripping level. Try to position the hole so it will be accessible when the camera is screwed down, and angle it away from the tripod-screw hole.

KEY-CHAIN TAB IMPROVES ZIPPER: If the zipper on your gadget bag is sticking, stop fighting with it. Just attach a key chain with an ornamental tab of your choice, and you'll be able to get a good grip on the zipper tab for a strong pull without fumbling.

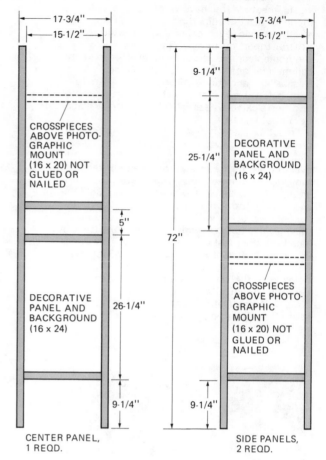

CROSSPIECES ABOVE PHOTO-GRAPHIC MOUNT (16 x 20) NOT GLUED OR NAILED

17-3/4"

15-1/2"

5"

DECORATIVE PANEL AND BACKGROUND (16 x 24)

26-1/4"

9-1/4"

**CENTER PANEL,
1 REQD.**

17-3/4"

15-1/2"

9-1/4"

DECORATIVE PANEL AND BACKGROUND (16 x 24)

25-1/4"

72"

CROSSPIECES ABOVE PHOTO-GRAPHIC MOUNT (16 x 20) NOT GLUED OR NAILED

9-1/4"

**SIDE PANELS,
2 REQD.**

DETAIL OF CROSSPIECE

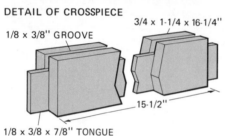

1/8 x 3/8" GROOVE

3/4 x 1-1/4 x 16-1/4"

15-1/2"

1/8 x 3/8 x 7/8" TONGUE

FOLDING SCREEN DISPLAYS PHOTOS: This folding screen serves as both a room divider and a display for photographs—and the photos are easily changed.

Construction is simple, with each section built individually, then attached with folding screen hinges. Materials are readily cut from 1x2 stock, and can be cut for you by a lumberyard. Both the vertical and horizontal pieces have grooves 1/8 in. wide by 3/8 in. deep along one edge to hold the panels; the horizontal pieces also have 3/8 x 1/8 x 7/8 in. tongues to fit grooves of vertical supports.

Each section was assembled with glue and small brads, but the horizontal pieces above the photos were not glued or nailed, so the photos could be changed easily. Decorative panels are of 1/8-in. plywood or hardboard filigree, stained or painted before the watercolor-board backing is applied. Photo panels are 16x20-in. print mounts; the prints are attached by dry mounting.

A VIGNETTING LENS HOOD: Your lens hood should be matched as closely as possible to your lens' angle of view. Too wide a hood admits stray light that can cause flare; too narrow a hood darkens or "vignettes" photo corners.

To check for vignetting, mount the hood, open your lens to its widest f-stop, lock the shutter open, and look through the lens from behind each corner of the film framing aperture in the back of the camera. Darkened areas in one or more corners indicate vignetting.

To cure it, hold a pencil against the hood's inner edge and move it back slowly until its sharp point disappears from view. Mark that spot, trim hood back to the mark with a hacksaw, then file smooth and repaint the edge black to prevent reflections.

PRINT ON THE RIGHT HALF, leave the left half blank, and fold the paper on the centerline.

EMULSION ON THE OUTSIDE carries the picture, while paper's back surface, inside, is easy to write on.

PHOTOS MAKE NOTE CARDS: Turn your favorite photos into photo notes, and you'll get a lot more mileage from them. Cut 8x10 single-weight, matte paper into 5x8-inch halves (double-weight or glossy papers are more likely to crack), and print your picture as a vertical or horizontal on the right half of the sheet, so that it makes the front of the note when folded; mask off the unexposed half of the paper during exposure, to avoid fogging it. If it's a shot you're especially proud of, you can print it across the entire sheet and fold the picture in the middle; the recipient can fold it out again.

Since unmounted, single-weight paper has a tendency to curl, use print-flattening solution (or print on Kodak's "RC" resin-finished papers) and keep your finished note cards flattened between blotters until you use them.

FILM-TYPE REMINDER: Trace a film box's end flap on a scrap of aluminum flashing, and cut with metal snips (or scissors), leaving enough metal around the outline to allow three bent edges as shown (box end flaps slip in the open end). Bend with pliers, sand, and glue or epoxy on. When you put in a new roll, slip the box end into the slot on your camera, and you'll never have to wonder what you're shooting.

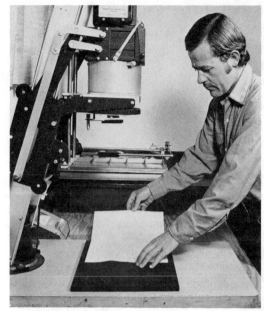

approximately two hours' time. It's just a piece of half-inch plywood that is cut two inches wider and two inches longer than the paper size it's designed for. (If you cut your paper to custom sizes—for full-negative prints from 35 mm, for instance—you can build the easel to fit them, too.) Cut three strips of metal edging (available from most of the better hardware stores) to fit three of the paper's sides, and mount them, flatside down, on the plywood base with $\frac{3}{8}$-in. x No. 4 sheetmetal screws. This will leave a small groove between the wood base and the metal edging that's intended for the paper to slide into. Paint easel flat black to prevent flare in printing.

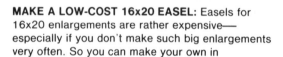

SLIP-IN EASEL (above and right) can be made to fit any size paper, is easy to load in the dark or under safelights. Black paint keeps reflections from fogging paper and reminds you to focus on blank sheet. Detail (above) shows how molding holds down paper edge.

MAKE A LOW-COST 16x20 EASEL: Easels for 16x20 enlargements are rather expensive—especially if you don't make such big enlargements very often. So you can make your own in

EASEL BECOMES COPY FRAME: An enlarging easel and a copy frame have the same basic purpose: to hold a piece of paper flat. So if you have an easel, you have a ready-made copy frame, too. To get the even lighting that copying requires, you can use soft daylight—wait for an overcast day, or

prop your easel up in the shade of a building where it gets even skylight, not direct sun. The easel borders needn't appear in your final print. You can move in closer with your camera to crop out the easel border, and crop out whatever is left of it when you make enlargements.

Color photography tips

■ MODERN TECHNOLOGY has greatly enhanced the acceptance and integration of photography into the average household. Today's 35mm cameras are so sophisticated that worries about focusing, exposure, and film loading are virtually concerns of the past. Thanks to automatic focusing, programmable exposures, and motorized film control systems, even the amateur photographer can take pictures like a pro with the mere press of a button.

As a result, photographers can concentrate less on the technical and more on the creative aspects of picture taking, such as composition and color. These are both personal choices and are subject to how the scene looks to you at the time.

To those not so artistically inclined, the term composition might sound a bit too complicated. Yet, one composes a picture every time one searches for a shot through the viewfinder, deciding to include some objects and exclude others, or to emphasize one main feature and blur another. Looking and actually seeing are two different things. Composition is basically seeing as well as structuring to create the information that one wants to convey.

Just as composition conveys information, color adds atmosphere to a picture. The bluish glow of a summer night sky, the harmonious blend of autumn trees along a country road can both be used constructively. Lighting as well as surroundings can particularly affect color and can create moods and ideas that are both vibrant and unique. Black and white, on the other hand, has a more dramatic effect and creates illusions that are emotionally striking, yet deceptively simple.

Moreover, photography can be fun and getting the right shot takes practice. So don't hesitate. Pick up your camera, load the film and go to it!

USE A WIDE ANGLE LENS to capture the near, wide, and far. To reduce the sun's reflection off the snow, use a polarizing filter which rotates to darken the blue sky without changing the other colors.

WHEN SHOOTING CLOSE-UPS, the best magnification and image size is obtained by using a macro lens. The macro captures both color and detail without destroying the subject when photographing smaller objects such as flowers and insects. This photograph was taken with a shutter speed of 1/125 at F/8.

THE TWO EFFECTS demonstrated here are called "framing" and "repetition." In this shot, framing is created by the colorful autumn trees in the foreground. Repetition is shown through the mirror image of the mountain seen in the lake.

SHADOWS PLAY an important role in this colorful rustic scene. The mid-afternoon sun creates a nice interplay of sidelighting and shadows without overwhelming the entire photograph.

FILTERS ARE one of the most useful and least expensive items in your photographic bag of tricks. They can be used for special effects as well as to correct specific problems such as haze. In this photograph, taken from an airplane, a yellow filter was used to darken the normally blue sky.

SUNSET PHOTOGRAPHS can be some of the most beautiful and colorful pictures you take. To achieve the proper exposure, use the camera's built-in exposure meter as a guide. Then, to be on the safe side, take a few extra shots using different F/stops on either side of the recommended setting.

THIS PHOTOGRAPH of an oak leaf in Autumn was shot with a zoom lens. For best results with a zoom, focus the image when it is seen at its largest size through the lens— at the lens' longest focal length. This photograph was shot with 400 ASA film, shutter speed 1/125 at F/8.

STAY AWAY FROM CLICHES. Unusual angles and vantage points add interest and drama to otherwise common shots, while retaining individuality and interest of subject, as in this view of Venice from a hotel room.

ANOTHER EXAMPLE of composition is seen in this pictur of a birthday party. Though there are other images in the photograph, their positioning draws the viewer's attention t the birthday girl in the center. (This photograph was shot w 100 ASA color film, using a flash unit and a shutter speed 1/60, at F/8.)

IN THIS PHOTOGRAPH, the viewer sees both an adorable kitten and a wood table. The photographer has filled almost the entire frame with the kitten in order to draw the viewer's attention directly to the animal.

THIS IS A GOOD EXAMPLE of a simplified photograph. Here the father and son together are the main and only subjects of the lens. When composing, try to minimize all distractions from the main subject of the photograph by selective focusing and cropping in the viewfinder.

GOOD LIGHTING is important for any clear, well-focused picture. Here, the photographer has positioned himself in such a way that the strong sunlight has created dark shadows across the subject's face.

ACTION SHOTS take time to master, but you can have lots of fun learning. To stop the action, use high speed film and a high shutter speed, and pan the camera along with the moving object. (This photograph was shot with shutter speed of 1/125, between F/8 and F/11.)

ABSTRACT REPETITION is demonstrated in this photograph. All of these beach houses are similar in construction yet different in color. This photo is a result of looking at an ordinary setting in a creative way.

THIS CARNIVAL SHOT was taken at night using 400 ASA film. To take night photographs such as this one, one needs to support the camera on a tripod or monopod. You will need to expose the film longer by keeping the shutter open for at least 30 seconds, and probably longer depending on the speed of your film.

THE OBJECTS in this picture have similar brown tones. Yet, three-dimensional depth has been retained, largely through the use of dramatic sidelighting. Experiment with single-color ideas to see how they compare to multi-color subjects.

THE IMAGINATIVE PHOTOGRAPHER can create abstract shots like these colorful pencils. Simply arrange the objects side by side and shoot at close range. A creative eye can transform ordinary objects into unique, abstract photographs.

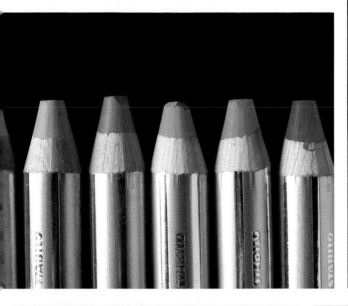

THESE SKEINS OF YARN were shot through a store window. A polarizing filter reduced the glare that is normally reflected from any window. Without the filter, the glare would interfere with the shot and the clarity of the photo would be lost.

BY BEING AWARE of your surroundings, you and your camera will never run out of available subjects. This simple door makes for an interesting abstract design. Judicious cropping isolates the most interesting feature of an otherwise ordinary subject.

DON'T STOP SHOOTING after dark. Night photography demands long exposures, so you'll need a tripod and cable release to keep the camera steady. To create these traffic patterns the shutter was set to the "B" mode and left open for over one minute.

A WIDE ANGLE LENS was used to photograph the graffiti on this wall. When shooting a broad area at close range the photographer should use a 28mm or shorter focal-length lens which allows for a wider field of view. Keep the camera level to minimize distraction.

SINK STOPPER STOPS STAINS: A large, flat rubber sink stopper, like the one shown here, makes a good coaster to catch drops of developer that may run down the sides of your tank or beaker and stain your darkroom benchtop. (Regular coasters are far too small for this.) Look for a stopper with a flat top, as many have central humps which you must otherwise cut off.

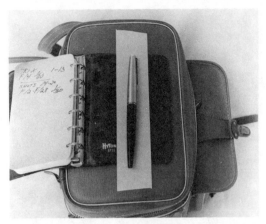

TAPE HOLDS PHOTO NOTEBOOK HANDY: Keep a notebook for recording exposures, filters, locations and other picture-taking information handy by taping it to the top of your gadget bag. The notebook is always easy to find, and the bag's top makes a good, portable writing desk. When in a hurry, you can take notes without even taking the bag from your shoulder.

CLOTHESPIN CLIP FOR THERMOMETER: A darkroom thermometer is easier to see if it's fastened with rubber bands to a plastic clothespin (wood ones absorb chemicals) and clipped to the side of your tray.

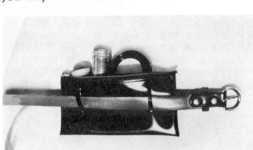

BELT CARRIER FROM A PENCIL CASE: A plastic pencil case makes a fine belt holder for small camera items such as extra film, filters, shades, cable releases. Cut two slits near each end to form loops to slip the belt through. The zippered case is easy to open and close with one hand while holding a camera with the other.

BLEACH BOTTLE SPEEDS TANK FILLING: Cut a thoroughly washed plastic bleach bottle in half, and the bottom makes a container big enough to fill your developing tank. Use a graduate to measure out the proper amount of solution, then draw a fill mark and label the volume on the outside with a brush pen or felt marker. The thin plastic feels flimsy, but when you pour, it conveniently deforms to make its own pouring lip. The bottle's upper half makes a handy funnel, complete with a convenient handle. Two gadgets from one bottle!

JUG KEEPS FILM COOL: A wide-mouth, insulated jug can keep your film cool in the summer and warm in the winter. The plastic-foam type is best because of its light weight. Just keep the jug open in your airconditioned or heated room at night, and close it in the morning.

MAKESHIFT COPY STAND : A vise and clipboard make a good, impromptu copy stand. Use a rubber band to hold the bottom of the paper flat to the board.

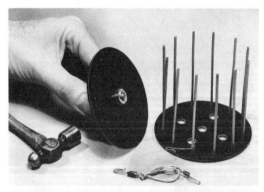

MINI-REEL FOR SMALL FILM: If your camera collection includes a subminiature pocket type using 16-mm film, you may find developing difficult without a special tank to handle such narrow strips in short lengths. An easy compromise is to make your own mini-reel to fit in a standard 35-mm tank. The one at left is 3⅜ inches in diameter and holds 34 inches of 16-mm film. Cut the end discs from Bakelite or similar material and the rods from ⅛-inch noncorroding wire. A short length of brass tubing or wood dowel makes a handle. The handle and rods can be cemented into holes in the discs with epoxy. Drill extra holes in the bottom disc to let developer circulate freely.

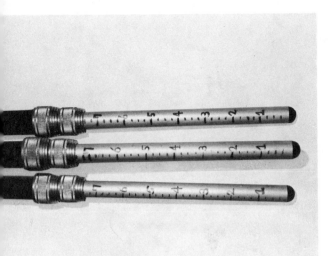

GETTING EACH TRIPOD LEG to come out exactly the same length can drive you up a wall. To eliminate this frustration, lay a ruler along your tripod's legs and lightly mark off measurements with a pencil. Using a small, pointed brush and quick-drying acrylic, paint each mark on permanently. If the legs are a tight fit, score the marks with a triangular file before painting; the paint will then be below the metal surface and won't rub off.

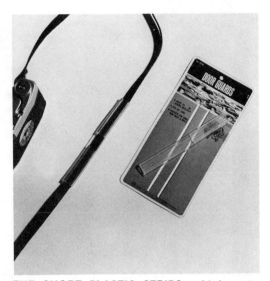

THE SHORT PLASTIC STRIPS sold in auto-supply stores as door-edge guards make good cushions for your camera neckstrap. Just insert the strap into the doorguard as shown, making sure the doorguard is centered on the strap and that the guard's cut area faces away from your neck. It will rest securely in position. Since the guards come in pairs, you'll have one for a friend, too, or for another camera.

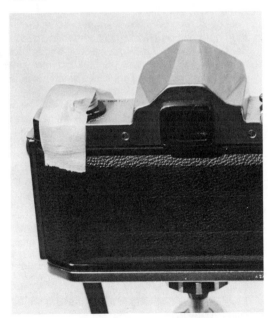

NOT ALL 35-MM cameras let you take deliberate double exposures; but those that do usually require that you hold down the rewind knob while winding the shutter for the second exposure. It helps if you draw up the slack film, then tape down the rewind knob *before* making the first exposure. Masking tape is fine for this purpose.

ATTACH YOUR SAFELIGHT to a pull-down reel of the type made for household light fixtures, and you double its utility. You can lower it over a tray for better inspection of developing prints, or raise it for more general illumination and to avoid fogging high-speed papers. This one is attached to a ceiling outlet, using a commercial type twist-lock electrical plug, but you can also mount it permanently, if you prefer.

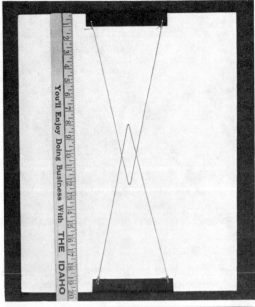

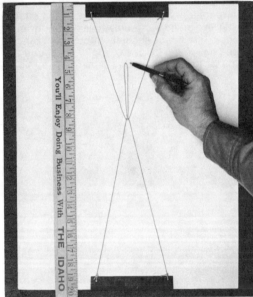

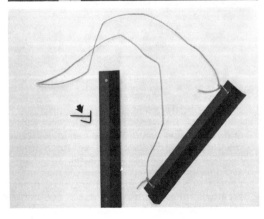

SALON PRINT FRAME: No need to frame your photos and display them under glass. You can show them more effectively, informally and inexpensively by borrowing a tip from the salon exhibitor.

First, dry-mount your photo on mounting board (16x20 is a good size). Then buy a strip of outside-corner plastic molding as shown (arrow) in the photo below. This usually comes in several decorator colors. An 8-foot piece is enough for about eight pictures. Next, saw the molding into 6-inch strips, and drill or punch out two small holes in the long leg of each, as illustrated.

Cut two pieces of cord, each 6 inches longer than the mounting board, and tie them to the holes as shown below. Center the plastic molding on the top and bottom edges of the board, turn the print face down, and pass the loop of the top cord through the loop from the bottom cord (left). Now pull the cord tight, and hang the print from the tip of the top loop.

If you standardize on one mount size, you can change photos easily.

The outside-corner molding shown will hold the print about ¼ inch from the wall. If you prefer the picture to hang closer to the wall, you can use edging, which lacks the outside corner molding's rear projection. For hanging pictures high on your wall, use an outside corner molding at the top of the picture, and edging at the bottom, to angle the picture downward.

Photo print mounting

■ GOOD REASONS to mount your photo prints abound: Mounting makes a print thick and keeps it flat, which protects it against curling, cracking and rough handling. But mainly, mounting makes a print special. It shows that you think a lot of the picture, and want others to see it at its best.

Of the many ways to mount prints, the best, in the opinions of some experts, is dry mounting, using a press or hand iron to bond the print to a mount board. Dry mounting is permanent, handsome and fairly cheap.

The simplest way to get a print mounted is to have it done commercially at an art supply store, framer or custom photo lab. But if you have a friend at an ad agency, a corporate graphics department, or an art school, you may be able to use their press.

For dry-mounting at home, the first requirement is a clear work space large enough to lay out your supplies, cut mounting boards, and set prints out to cool. Cover your work surface with cheap board.

You can't mount a print that's tightly curled. To flatten such prints, dampen them and redry them under pressure. A dry-mount press set at low temperature can speed drying and provide the pressure needed. If you stack prints as you press them flat, you need only dampen one out of three or four.

Cracks, stains, fingerprints and ripples (frilling) can mess up the edge of a print. To avoid these troubles when you're making prints you know you'll mount, center the image on a larger-than-normal size piece of printing paper, leaving a generous border all around that you'll trim.

For dry-mounting you need heat, pressure and dry-mounting tissue. The tissue is impregnated, like wax paper, with a meltable adhesive.

During the time it takes for your iron or press

MOUNTING TRICKS include centered-flush mounting (top; note black border around full-negative image); matting (above, center); use of "tacking iron" (bottom) to hold the tissue in place while mounting.

SOME TYPICAL dry-mount presses.

to heat, set the print on a piece of mount board and shift it around to decide what size the final mount should be, and where the print should sit on it.

Basic methods

There are three approaches to this: *Flush* mounting carries the image to the very edge of the mount, with no border; the print image fights its environment, a good technique for journalistic or other dynamic shots. *Centered* mounting is more formal, with a border (often a raised "mat") surrounding the image; usually both sides and the top are the same width, and the bottom is a bit wider, but some pictures seem to look cramped if you don't widen the top border. *Centered-flush* mounting runs the printing paper to the edge of the mount, but leaves the image centered; to keep the borders white, you'll need a cropping easel, unless you're printing the whole negative. Many photographers widen their en-

largers' negative carriers with a file so that light shining through the clear film borders around the image area will leave a black outline.

You can now rough-trim it to within an inch of the area to be mounted. The mounting board should be cut to the same size as the rough-trimmed print for flush or centered-flush mounting; for centered mounting, leave generous borders. If you're going to frame or mat the print, make sure the mount board size is measured in whole inches to allow the use of precut frames.

Measuring and cutting

To measure, use a rigid ruler and start at the one-inch mark, remembering to subtract one inch from the result.

For cutting, lay a heavy metal straightedge (other materials can be cut into) across the mount or print so the measurement dots just peep out from under its edge; a wide strip of masking tape stuck to the bottom of the straightedge will help keep it from slipping. Arrange the work so that you're in a comfortable position, with bright, nonglaring light and so that the blade will cut into waste area if it slips.

The best way to cut prints is with a single-edged razor blade, held with its surface perpendicular to the print and its edge entering the cut at about a 30° angle. Cut with a smooth, light touch.

To cut mount board, use a mat knife or a razor blade in a holder. Change blades frequently—dull blades tear as they cut.

Put print and board in the hot press about a minute to dry them out and reduce curl. Open the press at least once to let dry air in.

Cut a piece of dry-mount tissue the same size as the rough-trimmed print. Set the print face down and make sure it's completely clean and dust free—if you don't, you'll see how large a bump a tiny piece of grit can make. Put the tissue on back of the print and tack it down with a short stroke of the iron from the center of the print toward one corner, to keep it from shifting. Don't press hard, or you may leave a ridge in the print. A tacking iron (drawn toward you, not to its point) made for this is best, but you can also use a corner of a mounting press or the tip of a clothes iron.

Use the right heat

Your iron should be just hot enough to tack the tissue, not hot enough to melt the tissue over the iron. Practice on waste stock, first, waiting a few minutes after each heat-setting change.

Now that they're tacked together, trim print

and tissue to the exact edge of the image you want to see. Position the trimmed print on the board by eye, moving it until you like the way it looks. Then check with the ruler that the side borders are equal and the print is square to the board edge. Gently lift the untacked corner of the print, and slide the iron underneath to tack the tissue to the board: If you have a mounting press, protect the face of the print with a sheet of clean, smooth, porous paper and insert the covered print into a sandwich of mounting boards or hardboard till the sandwich is thick enough for the press to apply maximun pressure.

To set press temperature properly, start with a medium heat, insert a single-weight, nonresin-coated scrap print tacked to a two-ply mount board, close the press without locking it, count five seconds, then remove. The print should lie flat, with its edges lifted, and should peel off when the board is flexed. If it doesn't lift off, the press is too hot; if it doesn't even flatten out, it's too cold. Once you find the right temperature setting, a permanent mounting should take about 15 to 20 seconds with the press locked shut. Thicker, glossier and larger things require higher mount temperatures and longer times; RC prints and special tissues recommended for them require lower temperatures and shorter times.

If you're using a clothes iron, use it dry (no steam), set it to "synthetic" and use the low-temperature RC-type tissues. Preheat the print and mount individually by covering them and slowly ironing all over. Trim and tack as above. To mount, iron one swath at a time, heating first by ironing gently from the center toward one edge for several passes before pressing firmly. Keep the iron moving, and don't let the cover sheet shift. Check each as it is completed. Work toward each edge, then toward the corners. When mounting is finished, the print should lie perfectly flat.

Ridges and bubbles in the mounted print may be eliminated by reinserting in the press or reironing, first with gentle pressure to heat the affected area thoroughly, then with very high pressure to flatten it down.

The tissue is soft when the print comes out of the press; to reduce edge-lifting, cool it under the pressure of piles of books with newspapers protecting the print.

Mount boards come in several types from art supply stores and large stationers in a variety of sizes, finishes, colors and substances.

Illustration board, a quality paper surface on a pulp core, is the choice for most work. Thicker, four-ply board is better than two-ply for large mounts or when the print will get a lot of handling. Museum board is a premium type whose composition varies: The best is 100-percent natural cotton fiber throughout, but there are also cotton-faced pulp-core boards, and boards faced with acid-free sulphite. Your board and pictures will last longest with 100-percent cotton board.

You can also use a piece of photographic printing paper, fixed and washed and mounted back-to-back with your print.

Matting

For wall-hung prints, try a mat. The mat's color and texture act as moderators between the image and the wall—you're freer to experiment with colors, here, as you can always throw the mat away.

Cutting a mat takes skill and special tools—you may prefer to have it done by a professional framer. If you do it yourself, be sure to measure precisely: First measure the image area and the exact distance from each edge of the image to the nearest edge of the mount. Sketch these on paper. Now cut the mat board to the exact size of the mount, lay it face down, and mark hole dimensions of the sketch, top to top, bottom to bottom, but reversing the sides.

After cutting the mat, if its surface is dark in color, darken the newly cut edges with a felt pen.

The print is now ready to be framed, but if you're going to hang it with clear plastic framing or edge clips, bind the mat and mount together with tape.

Display big panoramas from little pictures

then trim them later. The drawing shows how you can use a tree, pole, building or other identifying object to help guide you in matching scenes.

As you swing the camera to take in different views, pivot your body from the waist up without moving your feet. This will keep the camera in the same relative position and minimize dis-

■ HOW WOULD YOU LIKE to make a photograph two or three feet wide capturing the sweeping grandeur of a mountain view, a shimmering seascape or a far-flung city skyline? Such scenes are too big to put on one piece of film. But you can put them on several pieces of film and join the pictures side by side.

Shooting panoramas is often considered a job for a pro, but it's actually a simple process. If you can take one picture, you can take three in a row. The only thing you need to be sure of is that the segments will join together properly to form a continuous picture. Since you can't judge exactly where one scene will end and the next one begin, you deliberately overlap your segments slightly,

MATERIALS FOR SPLICING are simple—some tape and a razor knife. A paper cutter is handy but not essential.

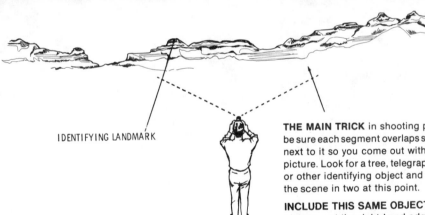

IDENTIFYING LANDMARK

THE MAIN TRICK in shooting panoramas is to be sure each segment overlaps slightly into those next to it so you come out with a continuous picture. Look for a tree, telegraph pole, building or other identifying object and mentally divide the scene in two at this point.

INCLUDE THIS SAME OBJECT in both halves of the picture—at the right-hand edge of the left-hand half and the left-hand edge of the right-hand half. Then you can use the object as a guide to join the two parts of the scene perfectly.

tortion. Try to hold the camera at the same level for each view, but don't worry if the alignment isn't perfect. Slight mismatches between views are simply trimmed off later. As a rule of thumb, locate the horizon line about a third of the way down from the top of the viewfinder and this will automatically keep the views aligned. If there is no horizon, use your identifying object to guide your positioning.

Wherever possible, make all shots at the same exposure. Minor differences in negative density can be adjusted in printing to keep the background areas close in tone so the seams won't show.

THIS SPRAWLING GOLF COURSE panorama was shot in two parts, requiring only a single splice.

1 **THE FIRST STEP** is to trim the side edge off one print. Make this cut through or near your identifying object. Now slide the trimmed edge over the adjacent print until you have a match. At this point, cut a slit at top and bottom, using the trimmed edge as a guide.

2 **TRIM THE SECOND PRINT** on a paper cutter, using the slit marks on the top and bottom to line it up. This will give you a perfect match with the trimmed edge on the first print. If no paper cutter is available, lay a straightedge over the print and trim off excess.

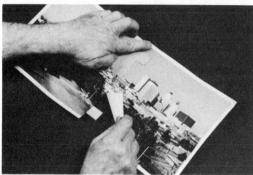

3 **STICK SMALL TABS** of tape to the back of one print so the ends protrude slightly. Let these tabs slide over the adjacent print while you're adjusting the alignment. When the match is perfect, lift the corners of the second print so the tabs slip underneath, then press firmly down.

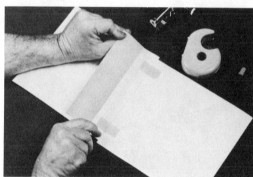

4 **AFTER THE PRINTS** have been temporarily joined with the tabs of tape, reinforce the seam with a strip of wide paper tape. This can be the brown gummed kind used in stores to seal packages, or you can cut a strip of stiff regular paper and fasten it with print-mounting cement.

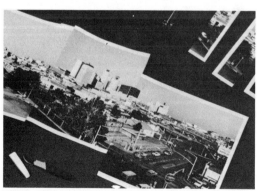

5 **JOINED AT THE SIDES,** the prints are now ready for trimming at the top and bottom. Note that the views do not have to be shot at exactly the same level. The discrepancy shown here was deliberately exaggerated to show that the effect isn't harmful.

6 **FINAL TRIMMING** eliminates ragged edges at the top and bottom and gives the appearance of a single photograph. Be careful to keep the horizon level. Lay a straightedge across the top of the picture and measure up from the horizon line at each end so trim will be parallel.

Add 3-D to your photo display

■ ORDINARY SNAPSHOTS take on a dramatic appearance when you mount them on blocks of wood, producing a three-dimensional relief effect. By varying the size and thickness of the blocks, you can create an unusual random-pattern wall display of pictures that otherwise get stored away unseen in a bureau drawer or photo album.

The blocks are standard wood thicknesses—¼-inch, ¾-inch (1-inch nominal) and 1⅝ inch (2-inch nominal). Three basic sizes accommodate 8x10, 5x7 and 4x5 prints. You can, of course, make the blocks any other sizes you wish depending on how you want to crop your shots. Trim off the borders and mount the prints on the blocks with a white wood glue (don't use rubber cement as this will bleed through, staining the prints).

The blocks are painted flat black to give a sense of depth and contrast. After the prints are cemented on, trim their edges flush with a sharp knife or razor blade and sand them smooth with fine abrasive paper. Then touch up the paper edges with a black felt-tip marking pen so they blend in with the blocks and become invisible. Arrange the blocks on a backing panel of ¼-inch plywood or hardboard. This can be edged with picture-frame molding or 1x2 strips to create a shadow-box effect to enhance the 3-D look of the photos.

The display panel shown here incorporates an added feature that makes the blocks easy to mount and rearrange. It's based on the use of

SMALL STRIPS of Velcro tape on back of each block make it easy to arrange pictures on panel covered with matching Velcro. Blocks stick firmly and can be quickly removed and rearranged.

Velcro—the two-part, self-adhering material sold as a substitute for zippers and buttons on clothing. One part consists of thousands of tiny nylon loops and the other part has hook-shaped fibers that catch in the loops. When pressed together, the two stick firmly to each other, yet can easily be pulled apart.

The looped Velcro is cemented to the display panel and strips of the matching hooked material are fastened to the backs of the blocks. All you do is press the blocks onto the Velcro-covered panel and they stay by themselves. You can move them around to change the arrangement or

add new blocks whenever you like.

Velcro comes in black, white, gray and various colors. Special cements for mounting Velcro are also available. Velcro supplies are sold at many department stores, sewing centers and fabric shops.

If you don't wish to use the Velcro, you can attach the blocks with either screws from the rear or glue. In this case, lay out the blocks on the display panel in a flat position and make sure you have a pleasing arrangement before permanently mounting them.

MATERIALS for photo display include ¼-inch panel, wood blocks of assorted sizes, self-adhering Velcro material, special Velcro adhesive, trimming knife and a small brush for spreading glue.

BLACK MARKING pen touches up edges of prints so they blend in with black-painted blocks. Run tip along the corners, slanting pen backward so that it can't slip and mar the faces of the prints.

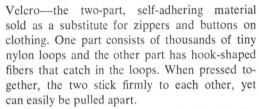

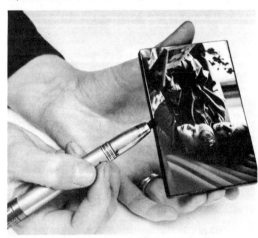

Picture-framing techniques

■ **Tools and materials.** Because construction techniques have been kept simple, the frames can be made using hand tools only. If you own power tools, the job will go faster, but the techniques remain unchanged.

Selecting stock. Standard pine moldings are the key to creating a good-looking frame; this factory-shaped stock eliminates the need for a router or shaper, or having to pay to have this work done by a cabinet shop. If possible, when you buy your moldings, pick out the materials yourself. Or at the least, take a sighting along each length of molding to assure its being straight and free of twists and bows. If you don't, you will quickly learn that warped moldings will give you trouble when you attempt to close a mitered joint. Also, avoid moldings that are excessively sappy; these will not take stain evenly, and you'll be disappointed with the finished product no matter how fine your carpentry.

Selecting the right frame for the picture. Since styles and tastes are constantly changing, you do have considerable "artistic license" when it comes to creating a frame. The basic rule to keep in mind is that the frame should complement the picture it will contain. Thus, a wide frame utilizing bold moldings is best suited to heavy, bold prints and oil paintings; narrow, simple frames should be used on small, delicate pictures.

To focus attention on a decorative object or display, such as the antique hand tools , use either an appropriately textured backing or make a frame with shadow-box effect (that is, with the front frame protruding an inch or so from the framed objects). A decorator rule-of-thumb (and in my opinion a correct one) is that *any picture will look good—in any room decor—if properly framed.*

How to mat. In general, delicate prints, watercolors and fine reproductions are enhanced by the addition of a mat. Mat board comes in 30x40-in. sheets in a variety of colors and textures from

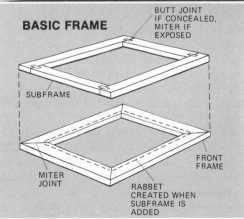

BASIC FRAME

BUTT JOINT IF CONCEALED, MITER IF EXPOSED

SUBFRAME

MITER JOINT

FRONT FRAME

RABBET CREATED WHEN SUBFRAME IS ADDED

BUTT JOINTS are used on the subframe and mitered corners on the moldings. The rabbet is formed when they are joined.

PICTURE-FRAMING TOOLS AND SUPPLIES

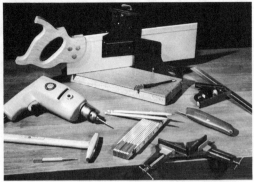

TOOLS YOU'LL NEED include a backsaw, miterbox, glass cutter, combination square, utility knife, corner clamp, ruler, pencils, nailset and light hammer. An electric drill, optional, is a desirable addition.

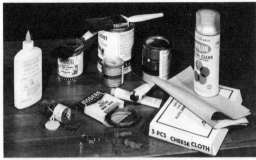

BUILDING AND FINISHING SUPPLIES: White glue, oil (or water) stain, varnish, assorted brushes (bristle for oil paints, nylon for latex), filler, paint, clear spray finish, sandpaper, cheesecloth, Skotch connectors, picture hangers, brads, picture wire and, for "antiquing," tubes of burnt umber and black.

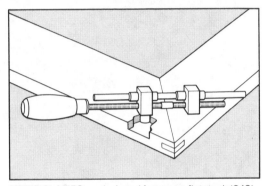

MITER CLAMPS are designed for use on flat stock (S4S). You must drill two ⅝-in. holes in back of the frame for seating each clamp. All clamps shown here are available at hardware suppliers.

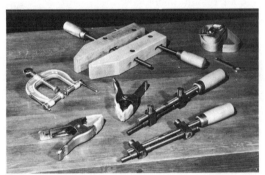

A GOOD VARIETY of clamps is nice to have around; they're a sound investment if you are planning to make a lot of frames. The clamps shown here are spring-type (center), three-way edging, handscrew, web and a pair of miter clamps—which hold a frame square.

smooth to grass cloth in shiny or dull finish. If you decide that your picture needs a mat, it is the first step in picture framing because its outside dimensions will determine frame measurements.

Two "musts" when cutting a mat: First, the bottom horizontal is *always* slightly wider than the top horizontal and the verticals. The average mat is usually 3 in. wide at sides and top and 3½ in. wide at bottom. Second, the cutout should always be made with the bevel cut. The sloped edge enhances the picture and also visually minimizes any minor irregularities if your cutting tool should wander from the straightedge even slightly.

Measure the picture to be framed and transfer the marks to the mat board. Make the cutout as shown, then decide the mat's width. Don't forget to add ½ in. in height and width to allow for the portion which will be in the ¼-in. rabbet. Cut a backing board, tape the print to its center and secure the mat.

As a rule, matted pictures are covered with nonreflecting glass. When you buy picture glass, make certain it is clear and free of any bubbles or waves. And, because picture glass is particularly fragile, handle it with care. Work on a clean, flat surface; preferably your workbench after it has been covered with cardboard. Take accurate measurements of the frame's rabbet opening, and don't forget to subtract ⅛ in. in length and width so that the glass won't shatter when you insert it. (If you prefer, let glazier do the cutting.)

THIS WALL GROUPING features a Charlie Chaplin and three other posters. Most are available at bookstores or by mail.

HOW TO MAT PICTURES

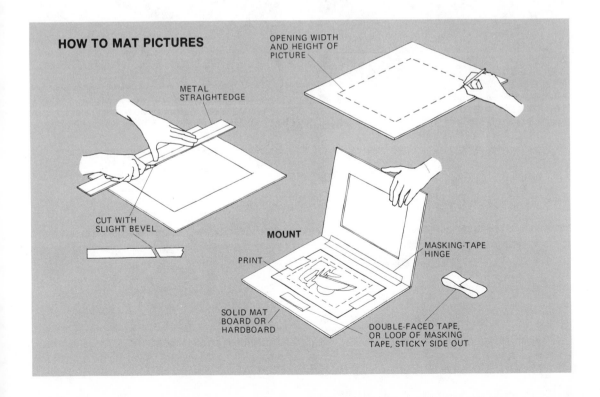

OPENING WIDTH AND HEIGHT OF PICTURE

METAL STRAIGHTEDGE

CUT WITH SLIGHT BEVEL

MOUNT

PRINT

MASKING-TAPE HINGE

SOLID MAT BOARD OR HARDBOARD

DOUBLE-FACED TAPE, OR LOOP OF MASKING TAPE, STICKY SIDE OUT

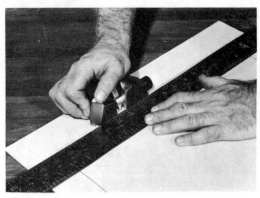

THE MAT CUTOUT should be made with a slight bevel toward the surface of the print.

THE CUTTER shown here lets you do this accurately and quickly.

Making a picture frame. Most frames have a rabbet to contain the picture (all of those shown do). In some cases, a single molding such as back band—used on a simple poster—does the job. But for more sophisticated frames, you make a two-piece frame consisting of a back (subframe) and front frame (with an opening ½ in. less in width and height to create the ¼-in.-wide rabbet).

A subframe can be joined using simple butt

MAKING A PICTURE FRAME

TO ASSEMBLE THE SUBFRAME, use glue and Skotch connectors on the back side. If the subframe will be seen from the front, use mitered (instead of butt) joints.

AFTER ASSEMBLY, drive in two finishing nails at each corner. Allow the nails to protrude ¹/₁₆ in. above the surface and then set them ¹/₁₆ in. deep.

CUT THE FRONT-FRAME molding using a miterbox and backsaw. For stability, clamp the miterbox to the workbench.

FASTEN THE FRONT FRAME to the subframe with glue and suitably sized brads. Molding overhang forms the rabbet.

joints if it will be fully covered by the front frame, Bainbridge board or cloth. If the subframe will be in view, however, miter-cut these corners as well as the moldings.

Use a miterbox to make the cuts and assemble the frames using a corner clamp as shown in photos. The clamp is fastened to the workbench and when the moldings are secured in its jaws, they're held square while you do the gluing and nailing. When all four sides are assembled, check the frame with your square and temporar-

ily tack two diagonals across the frame back to hold it square while the glue dries. Finally, set all nails $1/16$ in. below the surface, fill and sand.

Next, attach the front frame to the subframe with glue and appropriate-size nails. When the glue is dry, sand frame well with a fine-grit sandpaper and dust it thoroughly before finishing.

Finishing a frame. There are three basic finishes you can use: natural, stained and painted. Materials are a matter of personal preference;

FINISHING TIPS AND HINTS

TO "ANTIQUE" A STAINED FRAME, darken the corners with burnt umber. Use a clean cheesecloth to blend the umber carefully into the adjacent stained wood.

TO COLOR-TONE A PAINTED FRAME, apply a wash of the second color (above, blue over white). After a few minutes, wipe off the color with a clean cheesecloth.

MOUNTING AND HANGING PICTURES

AN OIL PAINTING on stretchers is held in the frame by driving 4d nails through stretchers into the frame.

MOUNTED PRINTS (on cardboard or hardboard) are secured in the rabbet with eight brads (two per side).

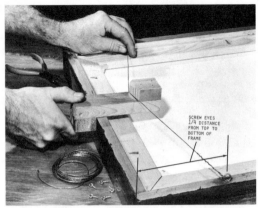

INSTALL PICTURE WIRE below the top of the frame so that the picture hanger on the wall will not show. A simple jig assures correct wire length every time.

A PICTURE-WIRE JIG is quickly fashioned from scrap. Distance A must suit the frame to be fitted with wire.

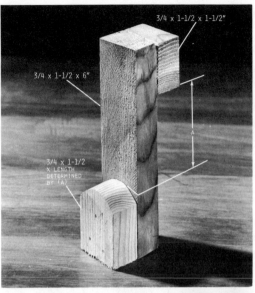

A STRIATING "TOOL," consists of 8d finishing nails through a ¾-in. pine strip.

TEXTURED BAINBRIDGE BOARD is used on some of the frames (from left): burlap, grass cloth and linen.

oils or alkyds give you a longer time to work the finish (when rubbing off an antiquing wash, for example), but latex materials let you do the job a bit faster and with less cleanup to be done when you have completed the job.

Natural finish. Apply either thinned shellac or varnish. Allow to dry overnight, rub lightly with 4/0 steel wool, wipe off dust and apply a second, nonthinned coat of the same finish. After 24 hours, apply wax and buff to a sheen.

Stained finish. Apply a stain of your choice, allow it to set 15-20 minutes, then wipe off the excess. Let this dry at least 24 hours, then apply a coat of shellac thinned 50-50 with alcohol. Wait

a day, then rub lightly with steel wool, dust and apply a finish coat of varnish.

"Antiqued" stain finish. Follow the same steps described above, but after staining apply burnt umber directly from the tube, using a cheesecloth. Corners and crevices should appear darkest and the umber should be carefully blended to "disappear" as you work it toward the center. Then, you can proceed with finishing as indicated above.

Paint finish. Apply a wash-coat of shellac (thinned 50 percent with alcohol) and let it dry. Rub lightly with steel wool, dust and apply color of your choice. You can use oil-base enamel or, if you prefer, latex. The latter, though, should be followed with a coat of varnish. *Caution:* use *varnish only* over latex paint or the paint will lift off. As you prefer it, the varnish finish can range from dull to high gloss.

"Antiqued" paint finish. After applying the basic color, allow it to dry overnight. Then, mix a black paint with appropriate thinner to a *slightly heavier than water* consistency. Apply this wash to the frame, wait five minutes and wipe it off with a clean cloth. If desired, the antiquing can be done with another color instead of black. Finally, proceed with an appropriate clear finish.

Spray varnishes. In general, when limited quantities will be needed, spray varnishes, lacquers and the like are easier to use than their brush-on counterparts. They eliminate a great deal of clean-up time and they set faster, which means that there's less time for dust to settle on your new frame during the drying time.

Hanging pictures. The easiest way to hang a picture is to use two screw eyes no longer than three-quarters of frame's thickness. Insert them about a quarter of the distance from top to bottom of the frame. Attach picture wire as shown and the picture is ready to hang. To keep picture from tilting, use a pair of picture hooks on the wall—spaced 6 in. or so apart—instead of just one. Make certain that the screw eyes, wire and hooks are strong enough to hold the weight of the picture.

MAKING YOUR OWN FRAMES is just half the fun; creating attractive wall groupings is another reward. This wall features old-time posters, a woodcut and tools mounted on burlap.

Picture-framing secrets of a master craftsman

■ WHEN AN EXPERT BEGAN making frames for the prints and photographs collected over the years, very few tools were used: a 10-in. table saw, a 4-in. jointer, a shaper with about 30 cutters, a vacuum cleaner and some small accessories. Gradually, additional items were added to do the job faster and more accurately. Following are useful aids that have evolved.

WEAR SAFETY GOGGLES

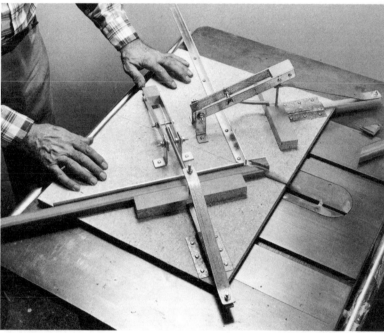

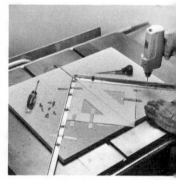

MITER JIG (left) aids in mitering frame molding accurately. Jig's spring clamp applies tension to sliding holding block to secure molding. To position jig's aluminum angle guides (above), abut the long edges of two accurate 45°/90° triangles over centerline. Tape them firmly in place; then tape guides as shown. Saw guard is removed for photo.

THE FIRST ITEM you can build is a miter jig. This aid ensures that frame members are mitered accurately on a table saw, so they will come together in a perfect joint. The jig consists of a base, two aluminum angle guides carefully positioned at 45° angles from the saw blade, and two clamping mechanisms that hold the molding being cut against the aluminum angles. This method of securing the molding as it passes through the saw blade eliminates stock drift and ensures its receiving an accurate 45° miter cut.

Each of the identical clamping mechanisms for the aluminum angle guides consists of a clamping block that applies even pressure to hold the molding against the aluminum angle, a spring tension clamp which works with a lever action to apply tension on the clamping block, and a clamp slide on which one end of a spring from the spring tension clamp is fastened.

To build the miter jig, first cut the ⅝-in. plywood or particleboard base. Two guides of flat bar stock or hardwood, which are attached to the base, should fit snugly in the miter gauge grooves of the table saw. They should slide without binding.

Before locating the aluminum angle guides, make a 5-in. saw cut centered on the base. Then turn off the saw. With a carpenter's square placed flat against the blade but not in line with the (set) teeth, use a sharp, 4H pencil to draw a line from the end of the cut to the back of the base. Butt the long edges of two 45°/90° triangles over the centerline (see photo) and tape them firmly in place. Then, tape the aluminum angle against the short edges of the triangles. Bore pilot holes and fasten the angles in place with screws.

Use metal shears to cut out the 26-ga. steel slide hold; a hacksaw will cut ⅛-in. bar stock for the clamp slide and spring tension clamp. Cut the wood parts.

You can bend the slide hold to shape with it clamped between two hardwood blocks (of the same size) held in a chinist's vise. One ¾x4x5-in. b should have a ¼x1⅛-in.-wide ce groove. On the second block, center temporarily tape in place the ¼x¾-in. stock used in the clamp slide.

Bend the angles that hold the spr tension clamp to the base by clamp the stock vertically in the vise—sho leg of the angle in the vise—up to bend point. Apply pressure with a we block to make the bend.

Assemble the spring tension clam as well as the clamp slides and we blocks. Locate the components on the base. Secure the clamp slide with slide hold. Secure the spring tens clamp. Install the screen door spring.

To cut moldings, cut the frame mo ing to approximate length before mak the miter cuts.

Make the first miter cut on the ri (short aluminum angle) side. Meas and make the second cut on the left si

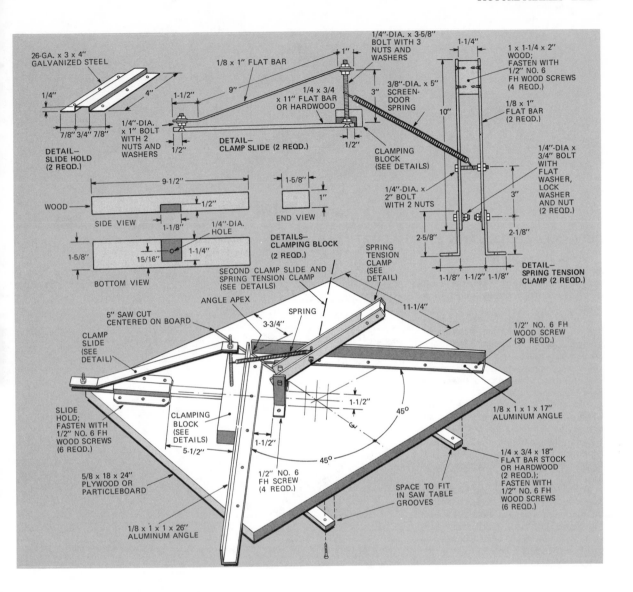

SHAPER HOLD-DOWNS INCREASE SAFETY

USING SPRING TENSION, hold-down and hold-in secure a frame strip in place for safe cutting on a shaper.

THIS HOLD-DOWN and hold-in, both on rubber casters, keep wood strips in place while they're being cut on the shaper. The hold-in rests flat on the shaper table and is held in place with clamps. Attach the hold-down to two 4x4-in. slotted angles with bolts and wingnuts. In turn, fasten the angles to the shaper fence with the bolts that came with the tool; or use 1-in.-long screws.

The slots in the brackets of the hold-down let you adjust it horizontally or vertically. To raise the hold-in, add a shim under it.

The holders are blocks of hardwood with rubber caster wheels. The wheels are cold-riveted to steel plates which are mortised into the wood block. A spring installed in the block at a 7½ ° angle and

attached to the casters causes them to press against the work as it passes through the shaper. After you have bored holes for the springs, a straightened paper clip with a small hook shaped at one end can grasp the spring and guide it in place through the hole. The free end of the spring is secured by a steel angle installed in the wood block.

To use the holders, position them so the wood strip being cut stretches the springs about ½-in. Push the work past the cutter, using a push stick. When the end of the strip arrives at the rubber wheels, move to the opposite side of the shaper and pull the strip completely through, exerting pressure in the direction of the fence to keep the strip from moving away and distorting the cut.

WEAR
SAFETY
GOGGLES

RIP GUIDE AIDS CUTTING

THIS GUIDE lets you rip several pieces of stock to exactly the same width on a table saw. Molding from one piece can be used with molding that is made from another.

The guide is made of a wood block that fits snugly into the miter-gauge groove; a movable, dimensioned crosspiece with a guide pad of plastic-laminate-faced hardboard abuts the work, while hardwood blocks on both sides of the crosspiece guide it.

You can set the crosspiece to the width of the molding desired and lock it in place by tightening the wingnut. After securing the guide from the bottom with a steel bar, carefully apply an epoxy adhesive fillet to the wingnut's bolt to lock it.

To make a cut, place the side of the board against the guide pad. Then move the fence firmly against the other side of the board. Back the fence away very slightly with the micro adjusting knob, so the board moves freely, and lock the fence in place.

SET THE RIP guide to produce a molding of the desired width. Adjust the rip fence so the work butts against the laminated guide pad, yet still is able to move freely.

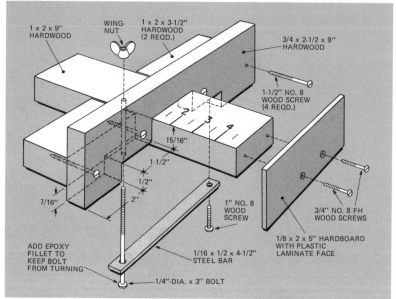

1 x 2 x 9″
HARDWOOD

WING-
NUT

1 x 2 x 3-1/2″
HARDWOOD
(2 REQD.)

3/4 x 2-1/2 x 9″
HARDWOOD

1-1/2″ NO. 8
WOOD SCREW
(4 REQD.)

15/16″

1-1/2″

1/2″

7/16″

2″

ADD EPOXY
FILLET TO
KEEP BOLT
FROM TURNING

1/16 x 1/2 x 4-1/2″
STEEL BAR

1″ NO. 8
WOOD
SCREW

3/4″ NO. 8 FH
WOOD SCREWS

1/8 x 2 x 5″ HARDBOARD
WITH PLASTIC
LAMINATE FACE

1/4″-DIA. x 3″ BOLT

STANDARD METHOD of ripping multiple pieces to the same width requires push stick and antikickback-finger.

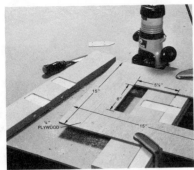

JIG GUIDE router with 5-in.-dia. base and ½-in.-dia. mortise cutter as it plows mortises for caster plates. Alter dimensions to fit router shoe.

FASTER GLASS CUTTING

THIS GLASS-CUTTING setup rivals the commercial rigs on the market. The cutter runs in a guide channel that is attached to a plywood cutting board. The guide channel lets you make a clean stroke with the cutter.

The base of the cutter is an oak block with a 1x2¾-in. center opening. The cutter rides on two pairs of ball bearings, each pair located on an axle installed in an axle block. The ball bearings used were taken from old hand tools, such as screw guns and drills. The tool handle is made of flat bar stock bent in a metalworking vise and fastened over the rear axle block; an oak grip secured with contact cement then fits within the handle.

An angle secured over the front axle block contains an eyebolt and wingnut. The eyebolt is connected to the center by a spring. The spring applies tension to the cutter when the eyebolt is connected. The glass cutter is bolted to a vertical wood block cut to receive the cutter. The block pivots on a rod secured to the cutter base.

To use the jig, align the left side of the glass to the dimension on the board's yardstick that you want the finished glass. Run the cutter from the top of the channel downward to score the right side of the glass. Place the scored side of the glass up on the worktable with the excess hanging over the table. Grasp the edge of the excess firmly, raise the glass slightly and crack it sharply on the table.

PLACE GLASS on cutting board and under guide channel. Cutter is moved from top to bottom in one clean stroke.

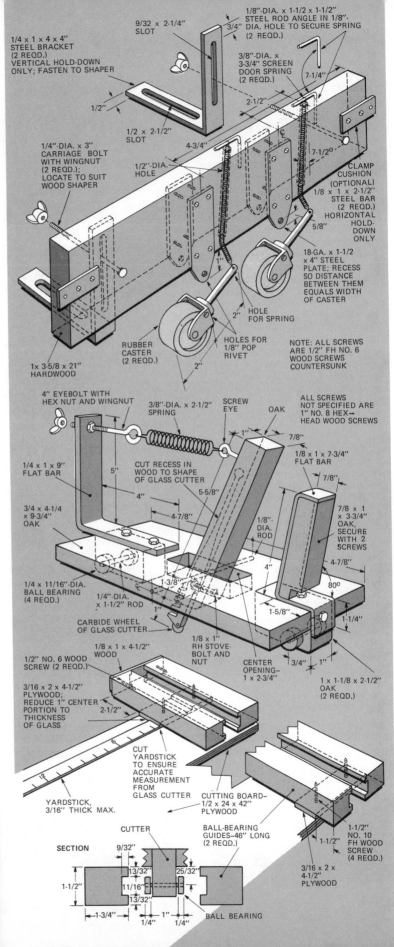

SPRAY PAINTER'S 'THIRD HAND'

The major parts of the holder are two pieces of wood held together by a carriage bolt, external tooth washer, flat washer and wingnut. The accessory hangs by a screw eye in the end of the shorter wood member. The longer member holds the picture frame impaled at the top and bottom of its rabbet on 4d finishing nails, their heads cut off.

The nails are installed in a pair of wood blocks. A drill press and sloping jig help bore holes for these nails to uniform depth. One of the wood blocks is stationary. The other block is secured in a sheetmetal slide positioned so the nails can secure the frame. Once the block is in position, you can apply tension to it by stretching a spring fastened to one end. The spring is covered by a rectangular aluminum tube to protect it from paint.

Begin painting the vertical frame members with both wood pieces of the jig positioned vertically. Swivel the jig to paint all sides of the vertical frame members. Next, loosen the wingnut and rotate the longer wood member so it is in a horizontal position. Then paint the remaining frame members.

You should build several of these jigs. After one frame is painted, return the jig to the original position and hang it on a nearby nail until the frame is dry.

The paint booth consists of a 16-in., direct-drive fan with explosion-proof motor installed in the end wall of the shop. Two curtains on rods are attached to the ceiling joists. The leading edges of the curtains have vertical steel rods in the hem. When you are ready to paint, extend the curtains and secure them with ties at the lower corners.

Selecting the right type of paint is sometimes a problem. However, if you're painting several frames in different colors, it's convenient to use spray paints. Antiquing frames can be done by using a solid blue with black glazing. A coat of solid gold, followed by a light spray of either red, black or light green paint also works well.

FAST AND EFFICIENT WAY to spray-paint a frame is to implate it securely on the frame holder. The horizontal wood piece is then rotated vertically to paint the edges.

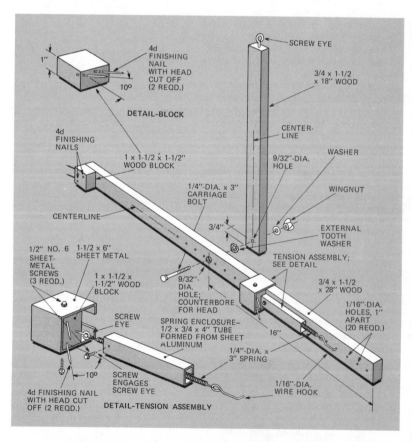

Floater picture frame

■ FLOATER FRAMES are a popular way to display art. The illusion is created by a groove running between the outer frame and an inner frame where the art rests.

Use 1 x 2 stock (actual dimensions will be about ¾ x 1½ in.) to make your frames.

First figure the size for the frame you need and cut the stock to four lengths for top, bottom and sides. Make each member several inches longer than necessary for the finished frame.

Then remove a strip approximately ½ x ⅝ in. from each piece by making two rip cuts with a bench saw or radial saw (Step 1).

After you remove the strips, use white glue and nails to replace them, leaving a ¼-in. gap or groove between the outer frame and the floater strip (Step 2).

Now miter each side of the frame to the exact size, keeping in mind that the picture will rest on the outer edge of the floater strip. Assemble the frame (Step 2) using white glue and 1-in. finishing nails.

Once the frame is assembled (Step 4), the nail holes can be filled with wood filler and the frame sanded and finished to suit. You might want to paint, stain or varnish the frame.

You can mount the art to a piece of mat or art board using dry-mount tissue or photo cement. Next cement the mounted picture to the frame's inner rim (Step 5).

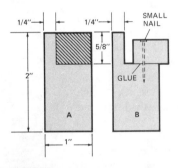

STEP 1: To make a floater frame, you will need 1 x 2 stock (the stock's actual dimensions will be ¾ x 1½ in.). Using a radial saw or bench saw, cut out a strip approximately ½ x ⅝ in.

STEP 2: Take removed strip (shaded area in A) and reattach it as at B, leaving ¼-in. gap between outer frame and floater strip. Use glue and small nails. Strip is blade thickness lower.

STEP 3: Miter frame members to size so picture perimeter will coincide with outer edge of replaced strip. Assemble frame with glue and nails.

STEP 4: Two frames are assembled, ready to be sanded and finished with paint, stain or varnish. Black paint in the groove will accent isolation of art and help give floating effect.

STEP 5: Mount picture on a mat or art board, then cement it to inner frame surface. Picture can easily be replaced by detaching entire mount and cementing new art in place.

Fancy picture frame repair

■ ORNATE PICTURE FRAMES with fancy overlays can be repaired even if much of the composition overlay is missing. All you need is one overlay intact or partially intact and repairable. The frame shown had corners which were badly damaged but one of them could be repaired by building it up with water putty so that a mold could be taken of it to recast the other three.

After the corner is repaired, it's surrounded with a wood form. You can use InstaMold (available at craft stores) to fill the form. It's a powder you mix with water to a fairly thin consistency so it can be brushed into crevices and valleys of the overlay without leaving air pockets. It dries in approximately 30 minutes, after which the form can be removed. Remove the form first, then gently lift off the mold.

Use water putty which dries rock hard. Mix it to a thick cream and pour it into the mold. Then place the frame corner upside down on top of the mold, press down to force out excess putty and leave intact for 12 hours. When you lift off the mold, a facsimile of the missing overlay remains which is difficult to tell from the original.

1 REBUILD THE partially missing corner as close to the original as possible with water putty. Let this dry about 30 minutes

4 CHIP OFF the old overlay to the bare wood. Then make undercuts with a chisel to help anchor the new overlay casting to the frame.

7 IF MORE than one corner needs to be replaced continue to use the mold since it shrinks as it becomes thoroughly cured

2 **ASSEMBLE** a wood frame around the corner overlay. Fit it as close to the picture frame as you can and dam with wet paper wads

3 **MIX CASTING** powder with water, fill the mold, let it harden. Then carefully lift the casting from the frame overlay

5 **POUR THE** water-putty mixture into the in-verted mold level with the top. Mix the putty until it reaches the consistency of thick cream

6 **PLACE THE** filled mold right side up under the face side of the frame corner. Press down into the wet putty to force out the excess

8 **WHEN THIS** much of an embossed overlay is missing, the overlay must be replaced with a new casting. It's beyond repair

9 **COAT THE** new overlay with a clear sealer, wipe the frame with a lacquer thinner, then spray the entire frame with a gold paint

Rustic picture frames from barn siding

■ AN OLD ABANDONED and weather-beaten farm building may be an eyesore to the country-side, but the boards in it are as good as gold. Weathered barn siding has become a popular and much-sought lumber for remodeling. The wood is particularly appropriate for framing wildlife prints, nature paintings and landscapes. Its rustic look adds charm to the picture.

A few pieces of this rough-textured wood can usually be had for little or nothing. The thing to remember when you spot a weathered old building on its last legs is that it still belongs to some-one and you should not just stop and help yourself. Get the owner's permission to remove a few boards. Probably he will be glad to get rid of them. Pick relatively straight boards and don't worry about nail holes—they add to the overall rustic look. If the boards are wet, they will have to be air-dried for a few days, maybe longer.

Some handsome picture frames can be made from old weathered barn boards. You'll need a miterbox and four picture-frame corner clamps. A table saw makes it easy to run the bead on the inner molding. Follow the steps below and you'll wind up with a beautiful frame that is a part of the picture.

AFTER CLEANING, rip boards 2 or 3 in. wide. Lay out picture size allowing ⅛ in. all around; miter to fit. Double check size. Butter ends with white glue.

PULL MITERED ends together with two-way picture-frame clamps and nail corners while the members are securely clamped together.

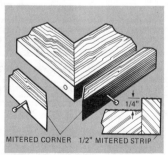

MITERED CORNER 1/2" MITERED STRIP

RIP ½ x 1-in. strips, miter ends and nail to outer edges of main frame. Gouge saw-cut edges here and there with a sharp knife.

ADD TO weather-beaten look of the frame by applying a light gray semi-transparent shingle stain. Brush with the grain.

WIPE OFF most of the stain with a coarse cloth; then while stain is still wet, brush lightly with oil colors that accent the picture's colors.

USE BURNT UMBER for rich brown tint, burnt sienna followed by a touch of yellow ochre here and there for a warm brown look. Experiment on scrap.

RIP ⅜ x ⅝-in. molding to shape shown for adding to inside of main frame from scrap stock. Sand the wood and miter the ends for an exact inside fit. The molding forms a rabbet for the glass.

PICTURE-MOUNTING TRICK: When covering back of frame with brown paper, dampen paper first. Then apply glue to frame and lay paper in it. When the paper dries, it will shrink smooth and tight. Use screw eyes to attach picture wire to back, placing eyes about quarter way from top.

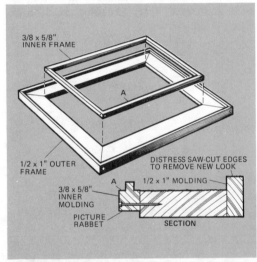

Labels in diagram:
3/8 x 5/8" INNER FRAME
A
1/2 x 1" OUTER FRAME
DISTRESS SAW-CUT EDGES TO REMOVE NEW LOOK
3/8 x 5/8" INNER MOLDING
1/2 x 1" MOLDING
PICTURE RABBET
A
SECTION

INNER FRAME adds decorative touch, also forms a rabbet for the picture and glass. Keep the shoulders of top bead on molding even with the textured surface of the main frame.

GLUE AND CLAMP inner molding together as a separate frame, using your picture-frame clamps to hold the four corners tight.

GIVE INNER FRAME two or more coats of a heavy white acrylic paint called gesso. You can purchase it at most art supply stores.

WHEN GESSO is dry, paint the top bead with two coats of gold paint. Finally insert the frame inside the main frame and nail.

Picnic furniture from chimney blocks

■ THIS SUMMER you'll enjoy your backyard patio even more if you add this handsome, contemporary furniture to the scene. Easy to construct, these sturdy pieces have low-cost chimney blocks for legs; a lot of high-priced lumber is eliminated from the project. Blocks used for the bench and seats were purchased at a local mason's supply outlet.

For each bench, you'll need 2 x 6 x 48-in. redwood boards and a pair of chimney blocks. After drilling a ¾-in. hole ½-in. deep, in each end of the wood (about 3¼ in. in from the end) drill pilot holes for No. 12 woodscrews. Next, using masonry bits, drill each chimney block for the anchors. Drill the block deep enough to insert plastic or metal masonry anchors. To make bits

1 **BENCH SEAT BOARDS** are cut to length, positioned on blocks, and ¾-in. holes are drilled through. Tip of bit marks spot where you drill.

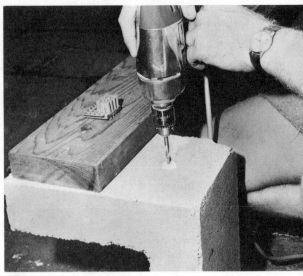

2 **HOLES IN MASONRY** should be bored in stages to make bits last longer. Start with a small bit and work your way up to the desired diameter.

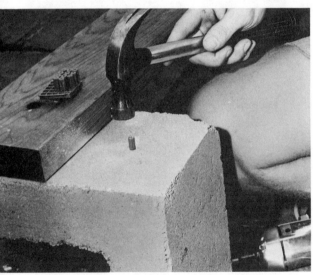

3 **MASONRY ANCHORS** are then tapped into the predrilled holes. One at each end was used here. Two per board at each end would be even better.

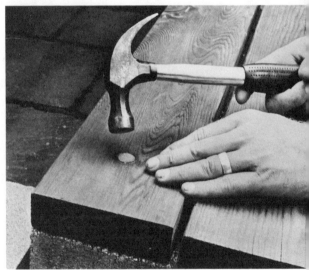

4 **FLATHEAD SCREW** is turned home in counterbored hole; ¾-in.-dia. dowel plug hides screwhead. Use waterproof glue to assure dowel stays put.

last longer, drill holes in blocks using several bits. Start with a small-diameter bit and work your way up to the finish size.

After pushing in anchors, attach seat boards to chimney blocks using No. 12 fh screws. Finally, to conceal the screwheads, apply waterproof glue to ½-in. lengths of ¾-in. dowel and tap in dowels.

To make the table, place two benches back-to-back atop two pairs of chimney blocks as shown in the photo. The table is sturdy enough without tying the two benches together, and you retain the flexibility of being able to take apart the table to create two benches.

To build the coffee table with slatted top, use

SLATTED COFFEE table is a slight variation of the furniture shown on the facing page. The ¾-in. redwood stock is separated by spacers, and the seat assembly is fastened to the blocks with galvanized screws and masonry anchors.

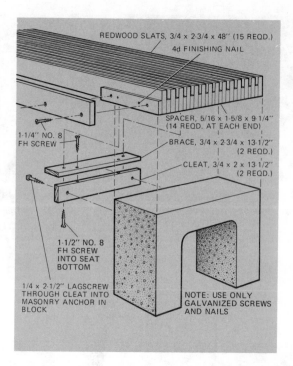

REDWOOD SLATS, 3/4 x 2-3/4 x 48″ (15 REQD.)
4d FINISHING NAIL
1-1/4″ NO. 8 FH SCREW
SPACER, 5/16 x 1-5/8 x 9-1/4″ (14 REQD. AT EACH END)
BRACE, 3/4 x 2-3/4 x 13-1/2″ (2 REQD.)
CLEAT, 3/4 x 2 x 13-1/2″ (2 REQD.)
1-1/2″ NO. 8 FH SCREW INTO SEAT BOTTOM
1/4 x 2-1/2″ LAGSCREW THROUGH CLEAT INTO MASONRY ANCHOR IN BLOCK
NOTE: USE ONLY GALVANIZED SCREWS AND NAILS

14 spacers at each end of the table to separate the 15 redwood boards. Fasten the spacers to each board with 4d finishing nails, and tie them all together with an L-shaped brace on the bottom which, in turn, is fastened to each chimney block.

For eye-appeal, give the blocks one coat of pastel-shade masonry paint.

Picnic table that folds flat

■ THE BIG PROBLEM with a conventional back-yard picnic table is that you can't put it away between cookouts. It's just too big to store—which means it's in the way when you mow the lawn, and it takes a beating from the weather. The latter means you'll have an annual paint or stain job.

You don't have such problems with this patio table. When the party's over, it can be stored in a minimum of space in your garage. With legs folded, it takes only 2¼ in. of space.

The table is sturdy when it's set up; the saw-buck-type legs are braced by their hinged supports. The braces not only lock the legs in the open position; they also lock them when folded—by using a pair of regular loose-pin hinges and substituting pull pins made from coathanger wire for the original hinge pins.

You can increase the size of the top, but if you maintain the 5½-in. dimension at the ends, you'll have to increase the length of the braces accordingly.

Block B is glued and screwed to the underside of the plywood top at its exact center. Although the braces are hinged to this block with plain butt hinges, you'll see in the enlarged detail that the braces are on the top of the hinge leaf and the screws are turned in from the rear side of the leaf.

The 1 x 4s, which are used to make the legs, should lap flush at the point where the members cross. To cut the dadoes at the correct angle, set your saw miter gauge at 11°.

Use three loose-pin hinges (six leaves). One leaf is screwed to each end of the braces. Another is screwed to each block A and the other two are screwed to the inside of each leg assembly. Thus, single leaves at ends of the braces engage the single leaves screwed to the legs as well as to those screwed to blocks A. To set up the table you pull the hinge pin at blocks A, swing up the legs to engage the hinge leaf of the brace with the one on the legs and replace the wire pull pin.

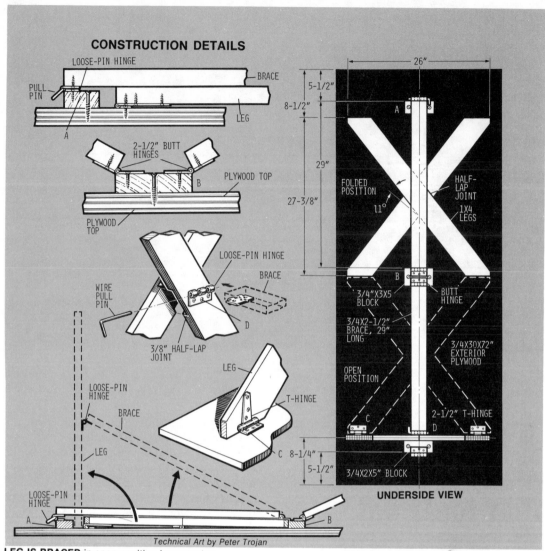

CONSTRUCTION DETAILS

Technical Art by Peter Trojan

LEG IS BRACED in open position by engaging mating hinge leaves and replacing the L-shape hinge pin.

Picnic table plans

ward carpentry project with no metal-working involved.

Since redwood has its own natural preservative, the only finishing required is a thorough sanding and a coat of redwood stain to ensure uniform color. Finish other woods with exterior enamel.

■ PLENTY OF ELBOW ROOM and attached benches are two of the most obvious advantages offered by the two king-sized redwood tables shown here and detailed on the following pages.

The hexagon design can be framed with 1¼-in. tubing, 1-in. standard pipe or 1¼-in. square tubing. If you don't have access to bending equipment, use square tubing and cut V-notches at the bending points, then bend and weld each joint.

The octagon model is a simple, straight-for-

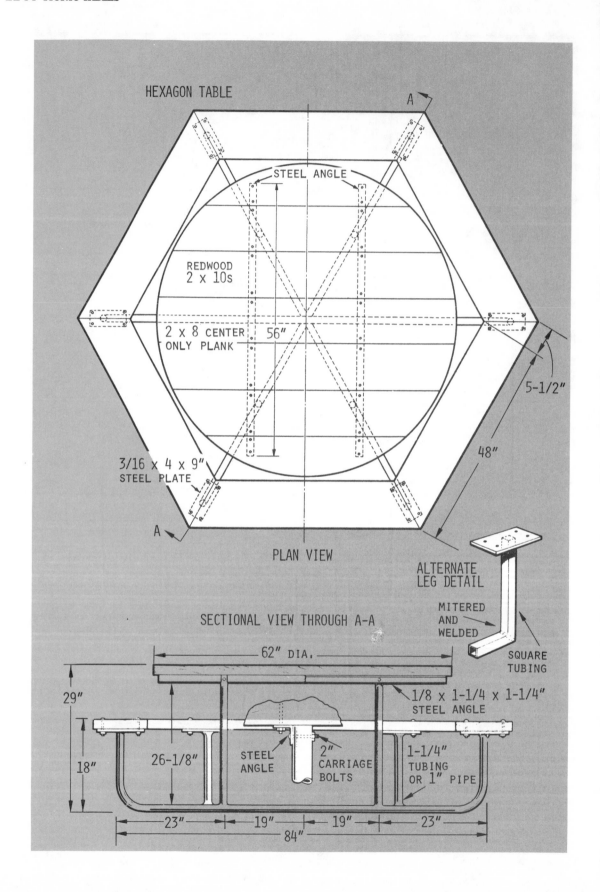

HEXAGON TABLE

A

STEEL ANGLE

REDWOOD
2 x 10s

2 x 8 CENTER
ONLY PLANK

56"

3/16 x 4 x 9"
STEEL PLATE

A

PLAN VIEW

5-1/2"

48"

ALTERNATE
LEG DETAIL

MITERED
AND
WELDED

SQUARE
TUBING

SECTIONAL VIEW THROUGH A-A

62" DIA.

29"

26-1/8"

STEEL
ANGLE

2"
CARRIAGE
BOLTS

1/8 x 1-1/4 x 1-1/4"
STEEL ANGLE

1-1/4"
TUBING
OR 1" PIPE

18"

23"

19"

19"

23"

84"

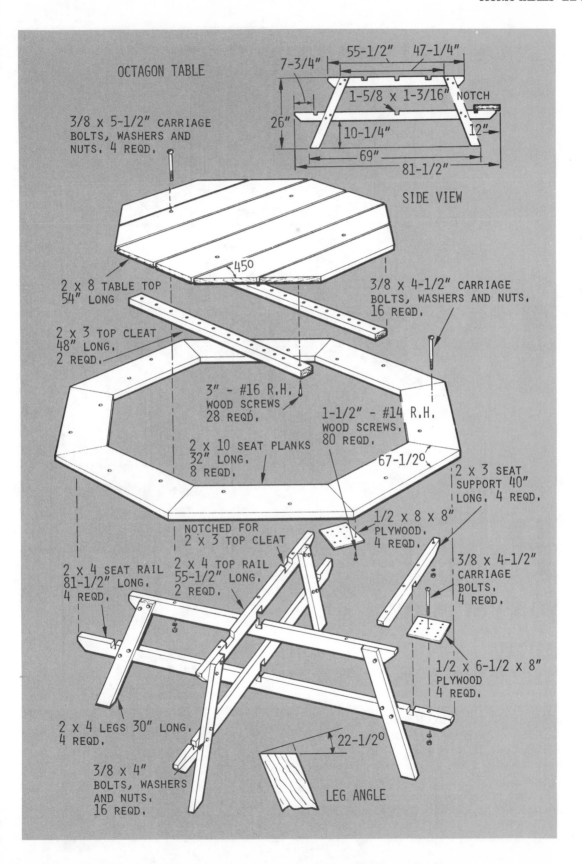

OCTAGON TABLE

3/8 x 5-1/2" CARRIAGE BOLTS, WASHERS AND NUTS, 4 REQD.

55-1/2"   47-1/4"

7-3/4"

1-5/8 x 1-3/16" NOTCH

26"

10-1/4"   12"

69"

81-1/2"

SIDE VIEW

45°

2 x 8 TABLE TOP 54" LONG

3/8 x 4-1/2" CARRIAGE BOLTS, WASHERS AND NUTS, 16 REQD.

2 x 3 TOP CLEAT 48" LONG, 2 REQD.

3" - #16 R.H. WOOD SCREWS 28 REQD.

1-1/2" - #14 R.H. WOOD SCREWS, 80 REQD.

2 x 10 SEAT PLANKS 32" LONG, 8 REQD.

67-1/2°

2 x 3 SEAT SUPPORT 40" LONG, 4 REQD.

1/2 x 8 x 8" PLYWOOD, 4 REQD.

NOTCHED FOR 2 x 3 TOP CLEAT

2 x 4 SEAT RAIL 81-1/2" LONG, 4 REQD.

2 x 4 TOP RAIL 55-1/2" LONG, 2 REQD.

3/8 x 4-1/2" CARRIAGE BOLTS, 4 REQD.

1/2 x 6-1/2 x 8" PLYWOOD 4 REQD.

2 x 4 LEGS 30" LONG, 4 REQD.

22-1/2°

3/8 x 4" BOLTS, WASHERS AND NUTS. 16 REQD.

LEG ANGLE

Picnic table you can stow away

■ IT'S GREAT TO HAVE a big table out on your deck or patio for those pleasant summer-evening meals. But finding a place to store it is something else. Often it simply stays outdoors all year.

Eighteen pivot points make it possible to fold this table into an incredibly small space of 2 x 5 feet, which means you can park it in a garage or basement with room to spare.

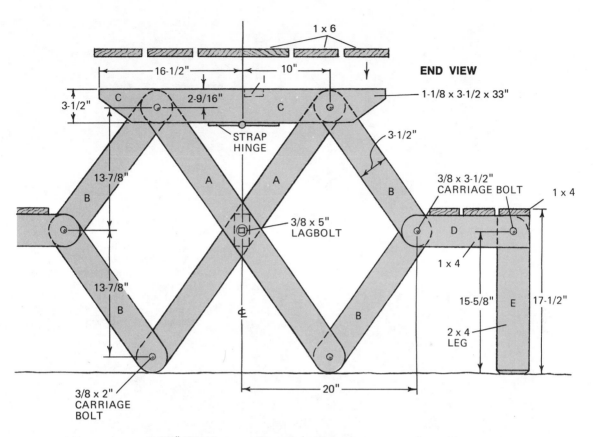

END VIEW

1 x 6

16-1/2"   10"

2-9/16"

3-1/2"

C   C

1-1/8 x 3-1/2 x 33"

STRAP HINGE

3-1/2"

13-7/8"

B   A   A   B

3/8 x 3-1/2" CARRIAGE BOLT

1 x 4

3/8 x 5" LAGBOLT

D   1 x 4

13-7/8"

B   B

15-5/8"   E   17-1/2"

2 x 4 LEG

20"

3/8 x 2" CARRIAGE BOLT

HINGE JOINT

1-1/2" NO. 10 FH SCREWS

COUNTERBORED HOLES FOR 1/4 x 3" CARRIAGE BOLTS

C

CARRIAGE BOLTS

5" STRAP HINGE

C   C

NEW HOLES DRILLED IN HINGE

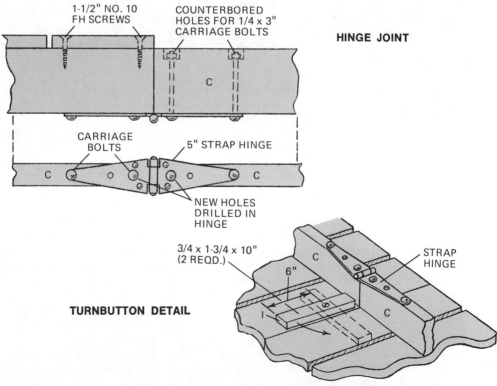

3/4 x 1-3/4 x 10" (2 REQD.)

6"

C

STRAP HINGE

C

TURNBUTTON DETAIL

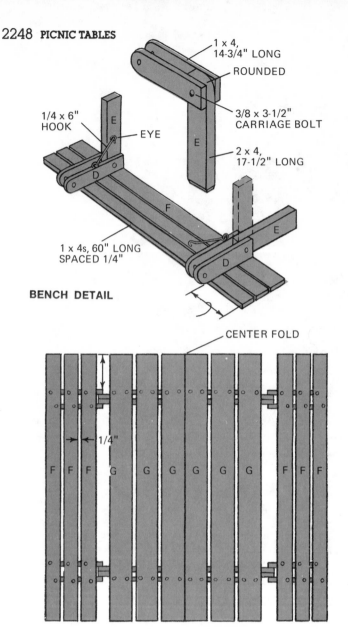

1 x 4,
14-3/4" LONG

ROUNDED

1/4 x 6"
HOOK

E

EYE

3/8 x 3-1/2"
CARRIAGE BOLT

E

2 x 4,
17-1/2" LONG

D

F

E

1 x 4s, 60" LONG
SPACED 1/4"

D

E

BENCH DETAIL

MATERIALS NEEDED (Redwood)

Key	Size	Amt.
A	¾ x 3½ x 38"	4
B	¾ x 3½ x 20¾"	8
C	1⅛ x 3½ x 16½"	4
D	¾ x 3½ x 14¾"	8
E	1½ x 3½ x 17½"	4
F	¾ x 3½ x 60"	6
G	¾ x 5½ x 60"	6
H	1½ x 3½ x 34¾"	1
I	¾ x 1¾ x 10"	2

Hardware

¼ x 3" carriage bolts	8
¼ x 3½" carriage bolts	4
¼ x 2" carriage bolts	4
1¼" No. 10 FH wood screws	2
1½" No. 10 FH wood screws	48
¼ x 6" hooks and eyes	4
5" strap hinges	2
Cadmium-plated washers	34

CENTER FOLD

1/4"

F F F G G G G G G F F F

E

TABLETOP

The prototype was built from long-lasting redwood. While it may look difficult, it's actually an easy table to build, mainly because all the parts are of lumberyard size. You just cut them to length.

The table is identical each side of a centerline. Each bench is alike, as is each scissor-folding leg. Spotting the seven pivot holes for each leg is done best by marking their locations on a sheet of plywood or wrapping paper and drilling the holes in the leg members to correspond. Round the ends of the members to a 1¾-in. radius and drill holes at the compass points. A good stunt to follow when rounding the ends and drilling the holes is to do two or more ends at one time by clamping the members together. This assures perfect alignment of the holes and makes for a neater job.

Cut parts C, to which the six tabletop members are attached, from 1⅛-in.-thick stock and join them endwise with 5-in. strap hinges. Drill an additional hole in each hinge leaf for a second carriage bolt. Use wood turnbuttons to lock the tabletop in the open position; place them on the underside near the hinges, on opposite sides of the centerline. You can keep the bench legs from being kicked outward accidentally by use of kingsize hooks and eyes, and drawing up the carriage bolts holding the legs snugly so the legs do not swing freely. Place three large washers between leg members at each point where the benches attach; elsewhere, just one washer.

Planters you can build

■ ONE OF THE quickest and least expensive ways to upgrade the looks of your home—indoors and out—is by adding a handsome planter or two. Three of the four designs shown can be used in either place. One, because it features a built-in bench, is intended solely for patio use.

Idea No. 4 is a clever, caster-mounted stand that is ideal for use beneath heavy house plants. Using it makes it a snap to move small trees and the like to sunlight, or for cleaning purposes.

Which wood to use?

California redwood is an excellent choice for planters. It boasts the unbeatable combination of natural beauty and good durability. Redwood is resistant to decay and to attack by insects.

When building a planter, choose one of the all-heartwood grades, such as Clear All Heart, Select Heart or Construction Heart. There are also grades available containing some sapwood, which run slightly lower in cost. These are available on special order from your lumberyard.

Use only noncorrosive nails to build any planter which will be parked outdoors. Conventional steel nails (common and finishing), when wet, will react with redwood's chemicals and cause unsightly stain streaks. To prevent such staining, choose aluminum-alloy, stainless-steel or high-quality hot-dipped galvanized nails. (*Note:* If you use the latter, remove any nail whose galvanized surface is cracked by an angled hammer blow. When the nail's galvanized surface is broken, it rusts like any ordinary nail.)

After completing construction, the redwood can be left as is. But you might consider doing some finish work on the planters.

Finishes

Use a water repellent on all exterior redwood. This is especially true for sapwood-containing grades. The application task is easier, and you will have a better job, if you apply the repellent before constructing the planter. Coat all edges, sides and ends of lumber. Be aware that using water repellent slows down natural weathering, but since it reduces the effects of moisture, it also protects the wood from dirt and grime. A water repellent can serve as the finish, or it can serve as the undercoat for additional finishes such as bleaching or staining.

If you do not plan to follow with another finish, you should apply a second coat of the repellent.

You can use a commercially prepared bleach to speed up the driftwood gray effect (that appears as a result of natural weathering). If you decide to bleach, read all of the manufacturer's use instructions on the label.

If you prefer a darker color, you will have to stain the planter. A pigmented oil-base stain can be used or you can choose a latex exterior stain. Either way, make certain the stain you buy is intended for outdoor use.

Do not use varnish or any other clear, film-forming finish on your redwood planter. Such finishes deteriorate rapidly when exposed to sun and weather.

Plants can be planted directly in a soil-filled planter or you can place potted plants inside. If you want the former, make certain that bushes and the like are planted using accepted garden practice. Plants, of course, must have adequate drainage: Too much moisture will drown a plant.

Roll-around plant stand

Dimension the stand to suit the size of your pot. You can make it by gluing up circular segments, or a block as shown. The latter permits sawing the skirt in one piece.

PLANT CONTAINER/BENCH COMBINATION

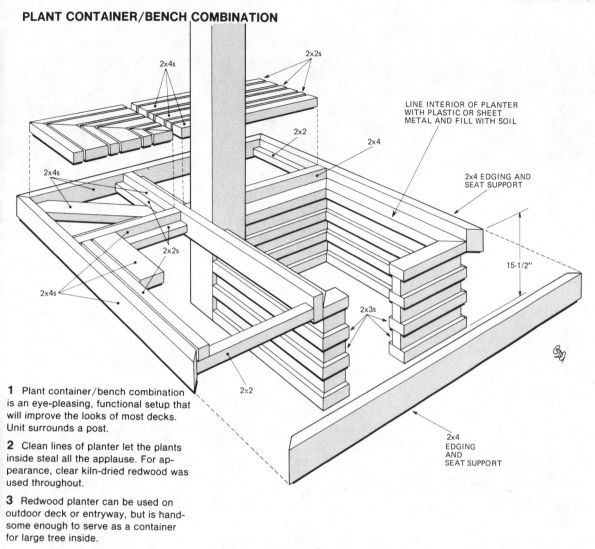

2x4s

2x2s

2x4s

2x2

2x4

LINE INTERIOR OF PLANTER
WITH PLASTIC OR SHEET
METAL AND FILL WITH SOIL

2x4 EDGING AND
SEAT SUPPORT

2x4s

2x2s

15-1/2"

2x4s

2x3s

2x2

2x4
EDGING
AND
SEAT SUPPORT

1 Plant container/bench combination is an eye-pleasing, functional setup that will improve the looks of most decks. Unit surrounds a post.

2 Clean lines of planter let the plants inside steal all the applause. For appearance, clear kiln-dried redwood was used throughout.

3 Redwood planter can be used on outdoor deck or entryway, but is handsome enough to serve as a container for large tree inside.

4 This good-looking and practical roll-around container, is intended for large indoor planters.

Make the block by sandwich-gluing 12 pieces of wood with joints alternately overlapped. For swivel plate casters (with typical 1⅝-in.-dia. wheels and overall height of 1⅞ in.), the sandwich should have two layers of ¾-in. stock with a ¼-in. layer in between. Drive nails in the waste areas to keep the glued pieces from sliding about when the clamps are applied.

Tack-nail two pieces of ¼-in. plywood to the block, locate block center and drive a nail through and into a board clamped to the band saw (or jigsaw) table. This serves as a pivot to make a perfect circular cut. Locate the pivot the desired radius distance from the saw blade and make the cut.

Next, remove one plywood piece to use as is for the platform. On the remaining two, make a

freehand tangent cut through the edge of the disc to get the blade to the inside. Reinstate the pivot and complete the internal cut to obtain a ⅜-in.-thick wall.

Glue the platform to the skirt, then add the ring. The spaces made by the blade are filled by gluing in thin filler strips.

Install the three casters with flathead machine screws and nuts.

The stand shown was sanded smooth, dusted off and sealed with a coat of shellac thinned 50 percent with denatured alcohol. Next, the surface was sanded with 180-grit paper, dusted and wiped with a tack cloth. To finish, two coats of latex semigloss enamel were applied; light sanding with 220-grit paper was done between coats.

BOX PLANTER

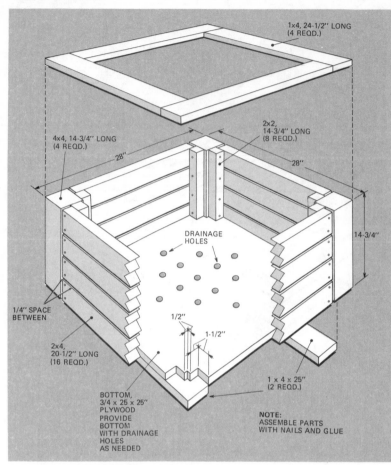

1x4, 24-1/2'' LONG
(4 REQD.)

4x4, 14-3/4'' LONG
(4 REQD.)

2x2, 14-3/4'' LONG
(8 REQD.)

28''

28''

14-3/4''

DRAINAGE
HOLES

1/4'' SPACE
BETWEEN

2x4, 20-1/2'' LONG
(16 REQD.)

1/2''

1-1/2''

1 x 4 x 25''
(2 REQD.)

BOTTOM,
3/4 x 25 x 25''
PLYWOOD
PROVIDE
BOTTOM
WITH DRAINAGE
HOLES
AS NEEDED

NOTE:
ASSEMBLE PARTS
WITH NAILS AND GLUE

REDWOOD PLANTER

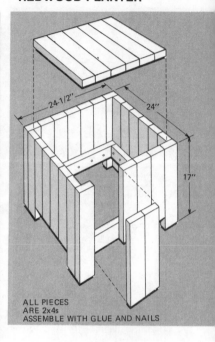

24-1/2''

24''

17''

ALL PIECES
ARE 2x4s
ASSEMBLE WITH GLUE AND NAILS

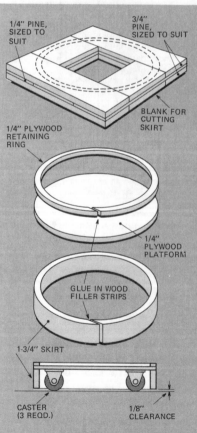

1/4'' PINE,
SIZED TO
SUIT

3/4''
PINE,
SIZED TO SUIT

BLANK FOR
CUTTING
SKIRT

1/4'' PLYWOOD
RETAINING
RING

1/4''
PLYWOOD
PLATFORM

GLUE IN WOOD
FILLER STRIPS

1-3/4'' SKIRT

CASTER
(3 REQD.)

1/8''
CLEARANCE

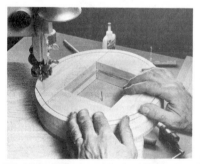

TO CUT circles from block, shift pivot point after tangent cut is made.

GLUE AND NAIL platform first, then add fillers and the retaining ring.

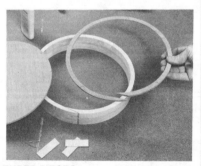

THREE PIECES are ready for gluing. Thin strips are used to fill kerf gap.

VIEW FROM BOTTOM: Three plate-type casters make planter easy to move.

Lighted planters: the way to grow

BUILT-IN FLUORESCENT lamp, housed in an adjustable light-box shelf, adds supplemental light in a most dramatic way to potted plants displayed in waterproofed base of this handsome table/planter.

■ GROWING PLANTS indoors is a fascinating hobby. Attractive flowering, trailing and foliage plants can be nurtured successfully inside the house with the aid of fluorescent and incandescent lamps. Plants can add beauty and color to your house all year long.

Plants need light to grow. Daylight in your home is neither uniform nor abundant. Fluorescent or incandescent lamps can be used alone or to supplement daylight. They make growing and showing healthy plants possible at all times.

Balance of red and green

In the dual-purpose planters shown here—a lamp table and room divider—fluorescent plant lamps give the perfect balance of red and blue light needed for plant propagation and reproductive growth.

Mounting heights of fluorescent lamps above plants vary depending on the number of plants used and their light requirements. Lamps are normally 6 to 8 in. above plants, and most plants need 14 to 16 hours of light a day to grow satisfactorily.

Fluorescent lamps are the best and most popular light sources for growing plants. However, incandescent lamps can supplement natural light or be used where fluorescents are not practical. Flowering or foliage plants needing no high light, do best under incandescent lamps.

Table planter

Movable pegs in the table-planter legs let you place the light box in three locations to adjust growth-promoting· light and warmth for the plants, whatever their size. Overall sizes of adjustable and fixed "boxes" are identical, so all parts should be cut in duplicate. The top of the light-box unit has notched-out corners cut by making two intersecting saw cuts on the table saw. Set the blade high to limit the amount of overkerf on the underside.

Use nails and glue

Assemble the lamp and plant boxes with No. 2 common nails and glue; use waterproof glue for the plant box, white glue for the light box. Drill pilot holes for nails and counterbore for wood plugs. *Special note on gluing:* Waterproof resorcinol glue leaves a dark stain, so you must scrape away any excess with a sharp chisel and wipe the area clean with a damp cloth before the glue sets. Use white glue for all plugs.

Round all outside corners and edges—most easily done with a router and ½-in.-radius bit. Sand all inside surfaces smooth before assembly.

Forming clearance shoulders

To allow ample clearance for free movement of the light box, plane the four 1¾-in.-square legs

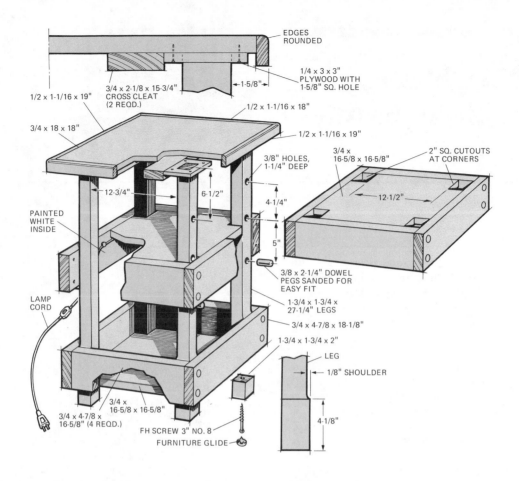

EDGES ROUNDED

1/4 x 3 x 3" PLYWOOD WITH 1-5/8" SQ. HOLE

3/4 x 2-1/8 x 15-3/4" CROSS CLEAT (2 REQD.)

1-5/8"

1/2 x 1-1/16 x 19"

1/2 x 1-1/16 x 18"

3/4 x 18 x 18"

1/2 x 1-1/16 x 19"

3/4 x 16-5/8 x 16-5/8"

2" SQ. CUTOUTS AT CORNERS

3/8" HOLES, 1-1/4" DEEP

12-3/4"

6-1/2"

4-1/4"

12-1/2"

PAINTED WHITE INSIDE

5"

3/8 x 2-1/4" DOWEL PEGS SANDED FOR EASY FIT

LAMP CORD

1-3/4 x 1-3/4 x 27-1/4" LEGS

3/4 x 4-7/8 x 18-1/8"

1-3/4 x 1-3/4 x 2"

LEG

1/8" SHOULDER

3/4 x 16-5/8 x 16-5/8"

3/4 x 4-7/8 x 16-5/8" (4 REQD.)

FH SCREW 3" NO. 8

FURNITURE GLIDE

4-1/8"

SET BLADE high and make two right-angle cuts to notch corners. Make such cuts so waste falls free to outside.

FORM CLEARANCE shoulders on two leg faces by making partial passes on jointer. Tape shows when to stop cut.

USE ⅜-IN. spur bit in a drill press to obtain clean-cut holes in legs for pegs. Dowels are lightly sanded for slip fit.

USE A PAIR of notched blocks and a C-clamp to hold leg for gluing. Apply waterproof glue such as resorcinol.

INSERT LAMP cord in bushed hole of fixture shell and connect the black and white leads in the lamp.

ATTACH fixture to center of light box with threaded nipple and nut. For safety, knot cord.

on two adjacent faces to make them 1⅝-in. square from a point 4⅛ in. from the bottom. Do this on a jointer and stick a piece of masking tape to the rear table to tell you when to stop planing. If you have no jointer, take a 1⅝-in.-square leg and add ⅛-in. thick pieces to the two outer faces at the bottom to form shoulders.

Bore holes for the pegs before gluing and clamping to the plant box. One C-clamp at each corner will do. Use waterproof glue and a pair of notched clamp blocks. Attach the 2-in.-long leg

extensions with glue and fh screws in counter-bored holes.

Top is built up

Two or more boards are glued together to build up the 18-in.-square top which is cleated (across grain) on the underside to prevent warpage. Facing strips, ½x1⁄16-in., are mitered and applied to the four edges, then the top corners are rounded with block plane or router.

The legs are glued to the top in ¼-in.-deep

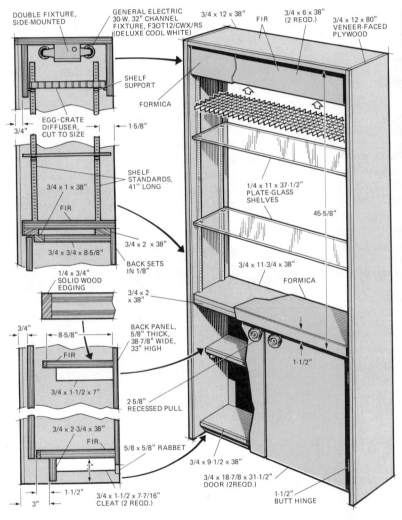

FACE EXPOSED edges of plywood with ¼-in. strips of solid wood. Use glue only, and clamp with masking tape.

INSTALL side-mounted fluorescent lamp fixture as shown; bottom-mounted type can also be used if you wish.

USE FINE-TOOTH plywood blade to cut "egg-crate" lamp-diffusing grid. Material comes in 24 x 48-in. panels.

wells formed by gluing and nailing 3-in. squares of plywood to each corner. Wait until later to glue the legs to the top.

Mount a standard circular fixture to the center of the light box with a pipe nipple and a fixture crossbar. You'll have to drill a hole in the side of the fixture for a rubber grommet, lamp cord and switch.

Finishing the table

Finish table with a coat of sanding sealer and two coats of satin-drying varnish. Apply two coats of bartop varnish to the inside of the plant box, and paint the inside of the light box matte white to help reflect the maximum amount of light onto the plants.

Now you can glue on the top. Place it upside down on your bench, apply glue to ends of the legs and wells and stand legs in the wells. Weight of the table will hold it until the glue dries.

Room divider planter

As a hutch or freestanding room divider, this planter makes a handsome display case for plants. Birch-faced, lumber-core plywood is used for exposed surfaces; common fir plywood and pine for the rest. The plywood will prevent warp, which might affect the fit of the doors. Use your portable saw with a smooth-cutting blade to cut the pieces from your 4x8-ft. panel. Remember to cut with the good side face down when using a portable saw. Guide it with a straightedge clamped in place.

All exposed plywood edges are faced with strips of solid wood, so allow for them when ripping your pieces for width. If you're planning a room divider with both front and back exposed, cut the sides 11 in. wide instead of 11¼ in. Cut all cross and shelf members 38 in. long, then butt, glue, nail and cleat them to the sides. Since solid wood generally measures ¹³⁄₁₆ in. thick and plywood ¹²⁄₁₆ in. thick, the slight extra thickness helps in gluing and adding strips. After the glue dries, you plane the strips flush on both sides with a sharp block plane, being careful not to cut into the veneer. A brad or two can keep the strips from shifting, and masking tape will hold them in the absence of enough clamps.

Use plastic laminate

Before assembly, cover the 6-in. fascia board at the top (both boards if the unit is to be a room divider) and the double-thick counter with plastic laminate such as Formica. The Formica counter surface will be easy to clean in case you spill when watering. Do the edges first, then surfaces.

Make a ⅝-in.-square rabbet along the rear edge of the counter and rear edges of the sides at a point from the counter down to hold a ½-in.-plywood back panel. Guide a straight-shank bit in your router with a straightedge clamped to the work.

Assembling the unit

To assemble, nail the top member first to the two 6-in. fascia boards and the bottom board to the 2¾-in. kickboard. Paint the inside of the top matte white. Next, start two nails through one side member at each of the four cross-member locations. Apply glue, drive home the nails within ¹⁄₁₆ in. of the surface, set the heads and fill. Now, with help, turn the assembly over onto protective wood strips on the floor and nail and glue the other side member the same way.

Check for squareness, then hold the assembly square with a diagonal brace across the back. Install the back panel that will help hold the unit square once it is in place. Finally cut, fit and hinge the doors with 1½-in. butts.

Rubbed finish

For a rubbed-effect finish, brush on a wash coat of sanding sealer diluted 50 percent with lacquer thinner. Sand lightly when dry and follow with a coat of satin stain. Even out the coat and lighten by wiping with a soft cloth. Work fairly fast, one section at a time. For a darker accent on front edges, brush on stain and omit the wiping. Then add two coats of polyurethane satin-luster finish. A polyurethane finish is durable and will stand up to water spills better than traditional lacquer or varnish.

Attach the fixtures

If you can't find a side-mounted fluorescent fixture, there's space for a conventional 36-in. two-lamp channel-type fixture with a T8 ballast. Fit it with two fluorescent plant lamps. Run the lamp cord through a hole in the cabinet top, knot the cord, insert a grommet in the fixture and connect wires. The plastic "egg-crate" diffuser is available at lighting and building-supply centers.

GROWING TIPS

Light intensity. Most beginners do not give plants enough light. As a result, their plants often grow and bloom poorly or have pale-colored foliage and leggy new growth. For more light, you merely bring the fluorescent tubes closer to the plants or add more lamps.

A good plant-lighting rule of thumb is to "provide 15 to 20 watts of fluorescent light for each square foot of plant-growing area." When growing seedlings, cactus or orchids, keep fluorescent tubes 6 to 8 in. above the foliage for strong light exposure.

Medium-intensity-light plants—African violets, gloxinias and begonias—should have tubes 8 to 12 in. above the foliage. Ferns and cuttings, the low-light-requirement plants, can be lighted 12 to 18 in. from above.

Duration of light. Flowering of many plants is controlled by the length of the daily light and dark periods. In general, short-day plants, such as poinsettias, chrysanthemums and Christmas begonias, need 10 to 12 hours of light a day. Long-day plants, such as the China aster, dahlias and annuals, need 14 to 18 hours of light to flower.

The indeterminate plants (12 to 18 hours) will produce flowers at all seasons. This group includes most household plants such as African violets, gloxinias, coleus, roses and carnations.

Temperature. A daytime-temperature range of 70 to 75° F. (nighttime, 60° to 65° F.) is recommended for development of quality plants. The cooler night temperature is important because plants gather their food during the day, but digest it during the night.

Humidity. The recommended humidity for most plants is 45 to 50 percent or higher. Often, in winter, homes have a relative humidity of only 10 to 15 percent. Cacti and succulents will do well under these low-humidity conditions, but other plant types will suffer.

You may increase the humidity by misting the plants twice daily with a water-spray atomizer, by setting the pots on trays of water-saturated gravel, or by using a portable room humidifier.

Ventilation. Plants lose water vapor through small pores on the underside of the leaves. Poor ventilation causes this to condense in a film on the leaf surface encouraging disease-producing organisms. To limit this, use a small fan or humidifier with its own fan to circulate air around the plants.

Plant spacing. Crowded plants result in long weak stems and encourage development of foliage diseases due to lack of air.

Soil. Since heavy clay and some other natural soils are not desirable for indoor plants, many hobbyists use commercial soils that are well aerated, provide excellent drainage and are sterilized before packaging. They contain shredded peat moss, vermiculite and perlite with added nutrients. You can purchase them under trade names such as Jiffy-Mix and Redi-Earth. Expandable containers for starting seeds and cuttings are alternatives to loose soil pots and can be purchased under the trade name Jiffy-7 Peat Pellets.

Fertilizing. There are many kinds of complete fertilizers on the market. A complete fertilizer has three major elements—nitrogen, phosphorous and potassium—and comes in dry powder, liquid or tablets. Follow the directions of the manufacturer, but remember, too little fertilizer is better than too much.

Watering. Many automatic watering systems are now available for indoor plantings, but the best method is still to inspect your plants daily and water them by hand when needed. Over-watering is the most common cause of trouble in growing house plants. Water plants in the morning when the temperature is rising. Use tepid water, not cold water from the tap.

From experience you will learn how much water each plant needs. Differences of size and leaf area, plant type, conditions of soil, and temperature of growing area will affect your decision.

Cuttings. A common way to start new house plants is with cuttings. A cutting is any part cut from a plant capable of producing roots and continuing growth, thus developing into a new individual plant. The cutting allows plants to mature rapidly and closely resemble the parent plant.

Cuttings of 4 to 5 inches can be removed from a parent plant with a sharp knife. Cut the stem just below the joint. As soon as it is cut, insert the cutting into a moist rooting medium such as vermiculite, perlite or a fine grade of peat moss. Keep medium moist until the cutting has rooted. Cuttings should be transplanted as soon as roots are well developed.

Seeds. Sow seeds as evenly as possible in a container having good drainage; then cover with a fine soil. Or use compressed peat pots, following the maker's instructions. Small seeds should be lightly covered, while larger seeds should be covered to a depth of twice their greatest diameter. Dampen the soil with a fine spray and cover the container with clear plastic or glass to maintain the moisture of the medium.

The temperature for seed germination should be about 10° higher than that required for normal plant growth.

The small seedlings should be potted or reset as soon as they are large enough to handle.

Hardening off plants. Bedding plants (flowers and vegetables) started indoors are soft and must gradually get accustomed to the wind and sun. A week before transplanting the garden, move the plants outdoors to a sheltered, shady place. After a couple of days outside, the plants will become stronger and ready for the sun.

Planters for your garden

■ SOMETHING DIFFERENT in the way of planters are these niches that are framed as part of the fence. Besides being a novel feature that serves to break up a long expanse of plain fence, the enclosures actually afford protection to a plant from strong winds and at the same time provide extra bracing to the fence itself.

A small bridge, such as the one below with its built-in planter boxes, will add charm to a fish pond and rock garden. When building both these projects from long-lasting California redwood, use noncorroding nails (hot-dipped galvanized, aluminum alloy or stainless steel) so the nails won't discolor the wood.

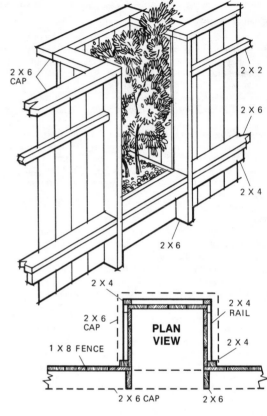

2 X 6 CAP · 2 X 2 · 2 X 6 · 2 X 4 · 2 X 6

2 X 4
2 X 6 CAP
1 X 8 FENCE

PLAN VIEW

2 X 4 RAIL
2 X 4

2 X 6 CAP · 2 X 6

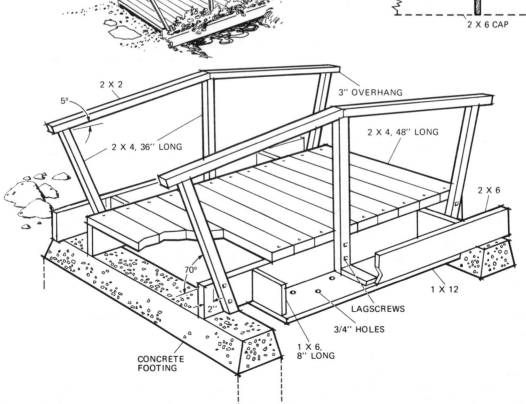

2 X 2
5°
2 X 4, 36" LONG
3" OVERHANG
2 X 4, 48" LONG
2 X 6
1 X 12
LAGSCREWS
70°
2"
3/4" HOLES
1 X 6, 8" LONG
CONCRETE FOOTING

Planters you can use indoors or out

■ HERE ARE TWO handsome pieces for showing off your prized potted plants. The contemporary bench-type stand features scalloped skirts which hint of early Americana. It's built entirely of pine. The hanging cubed planter is of redwood, and ordinary window sash chain is used to hang it.

Both of these plant containers can be used on the patio during the summer and simply moved indoors when cool weather arrives.

Use only hot-dipped galvanized or aluminum nails and screws for fastening. Ordinary steel fasteners will quickly rust and produce unsightly stains. The best adhesive choice because of exposure to weather is resorcinol glue. This is a two-part glue which is easily applied (after mixing) with a clean brush or wooden spatula. Caution Read manufacturer's instructions for mixing and use, and mix the glue in batches that will be used in your work session—leftovers cannot be saved.

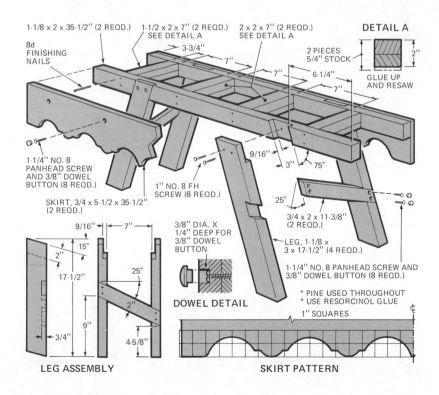

1-1/8 x 2 x 35-1/2" (2 REQD.)

1-1/2 x 2 x 7" (2 REQD.) SEE DETAIL A

2 x 2 x 7" (2 REQD.) SEE DETAIL A

8d FINISHING NAILS

3-3/4"

7"

7"

6-1/4"

7"

DETAIL A

2 PIECES 5/4" STOCK

2"

GLUE UP AND RESAW

1-1/4" NO. 8 PANHEAD SCREW AND 3/8" DOWEL BUTTON (8 REQD.)

1" NO. 8 FH SCREW (8 REQD.)

9/16"

3"

75°

25°

3/4 x 2 x 11-3/8" (2 REQD.)

SKIRT, 3/4 x 5-1/2 x 35-1/2" (2 REQD.)

9/16"

7"

15°

2"

17-1/2"

9"

3/4"

25°

2"

4-5/8"

3/8" DIA. X 1/4" DEEP FOR 3/8" DOWEL BUTTON

DOWEL DETAIL

LEG, 1-1/8 x 3 x 17-1/2" (4 REQD.)

1-1/4" NO. 8 PANHEAD SCREW AND 3/8" DOWEL BUTTON (8 REQD.)

* PINE USED THROUGHOUT
* USE RESORCINOL GLUE

1" SQUARES

LEG ASSEMBLY

SKIRT PATTERN

The bench was finished with an exterior stain and two coats of spar varnish. The hanging planter was left natural, because it is of redwood, and treated with clear wood preservative.

Bench-type planter

To save cutting problems through and around knots, use clear pine for the skirts. Other parts can be of No. 1 or 2 common pine.

Start by cutting parts to size. To make notches in the legs, use either a handsaw and chisel, table saw or radial-arm saw. Note that the crosspieces are created by gluing up two thicknesses of 5/4-in. stock and then resawing them to desired size. When all parts are cut, test-assemble using 4d finishing nails only. When satisfied, permanently assemble with glue and fasteners.

Hanging planter

A quickie project that actually is fun to make, this hanging plant container is sized to suit a good-size flowerpot. The design can be used for smaller flowerpots, but the blocks must then be reduced in length and width.

Cut the required number of blocks on a table saw or radial saw. Notice that each course of blocks is a slightly smaller size than the one above it. This gives the proper taper to hold the pot. Refer to the drawing for exact dimensions. Sand and dust off all parts. Assemble the planter upside down using glue and nails. Note: Lay out each course on the preceding layer, arrange blocks until satisfied, mark their positions, and permanently fasten them with glue. Insert screw eyes, attach sash chain and suspend planter from a stout S-hook. Install flowerpot.

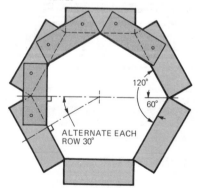

ASSEMBLE UPSIDE
DOWN WITH RESORCINOL
GLUE AND 6d FINISHING
NAILS

120°
60°

ALTERNATE EACH
ROW 30°

1ST ROW—6 PIECES 1-1/2 x 1-7/8 x 5"
2ND ROW—6 PIECES 1-1/2 x 1-7/8 x 4-1/2"
3RD ROW—6 PIECES 1-1/2 x 1-7/8 x 4"
4TH ROW—6 PIECES 1-1/2 x 1-7/8 x 3-3/8"
5TH ROW—6 PIECES 1-1/2 x 1-7/8 x 2-7/8"
6TH ROW—6 PIECES 1-1/8 x 1-1/2 x 2-1/2"

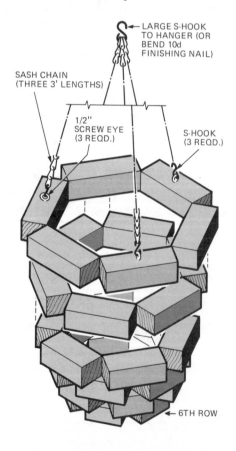

LARGE S-HOOK
TO HANGER (OR
BEND 10d
FINISHING NAIL)

SASH CHAIN
(THREE 3' LENGTHS)

1/2"
SCREW EYE
(3 REQD.)

S-HOOK
(3 REQD.)

6TH ROW

Tub planters

■ FOR HALF OR LESS the price you pay at a patio shop, you can make a pair of handsome, sturdy planter tubs by sawing a used whiskey barrel in half.

When you get a barrel, the chances are its metal hoops will be rusty, but a little elbow grease and a wire brush will soon get rid of the rust (an electric sander will speed the job). When you saw the barrel in half, you'll know it once held firewater because its charred interior will reek of bourbon. But this won't hurt your plants one bit; the smell will soon dissipate.

A homemade T-square with a thin bendable blade is used to mark the barrel around its cir-

ELECTRIC SANDER and coarse abrasive paper will derust the hoops in a hurry; or do it by hand with a wire brush. For a varnish finish, sand the staves for a new-wood look.

cumference, and a sabre saw will cut the barrel in half quickly. Drain holes are required in the bottom of each tub, and you have a choice of painting the oak staves or sanding and varnishing them.

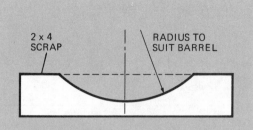

2 x 4
SCRAP

RADIUS TO
SUIT BARREL

BARREL STAYS PUT for sawing when cradled
with wood blocks at each end. Mark cutting line
around circumference, plunge cut with a sabre
saw, then rotate barrel.

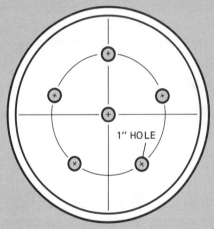

1″ HOLE

DRILL SIX DRAIN HOLES in the bottom of each
tub; when you're ready to add plants, place rocks
in the bottom, cover them with burlap and fill
tub with potting soil.

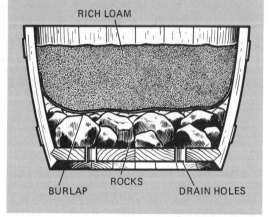

RICH LOAM

BURLAP   ROCKS   DRAIN HOLES

WEAR
SAFETY
GOGGLES

Wheelbarrow planter

■ THIS LITTLE patio planter is fun to build whether you are a dyed-in-the-wool wood-worker or a guy taking his first whack at a project. Douglas fir was used here but other material can be used. To start, lay out and make all straight cuts for the bottom, side panels and the two end pieces that make up the wheelbarrow bucket. Next, set the saw blade at a 30° angle and make the bevel cuts in the two end pieces. To keep construction simple, use butt joints for all assembly. Make certain that edges to be joined are perfectly square. Finally, cut the handles and the wheels. The plans call for all parts to be cut from ¾-in. (actual) stock. The wheel axles are 3-in. lengths of ½-in. dowel.

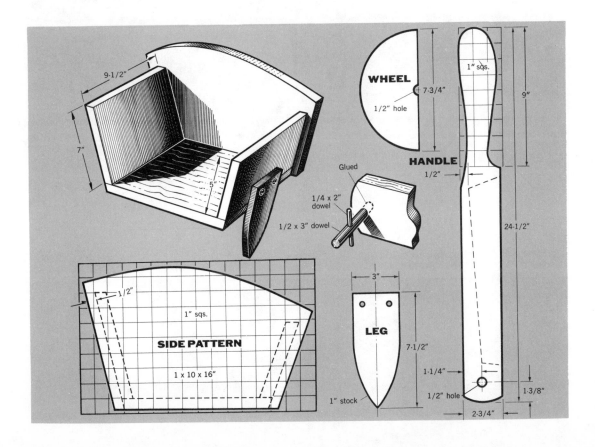

9-1/2"

7"

5"

WHEEL

7-3/4"

1/2" hole

HANDLE

1" sqs.

9"

1/2"

24-1/2"

Glued

1/4 x 2" dowel

1/2 x 3" dowel

1/2"

SIDE PATTERN

1/2"

1" sqs.

1 x 10 x 16"

LEG

3"

7-1/2"

1" stock

1-1/4"

1/2" hole

1-3/8"

2-3/4"

Working with acrylic plastic

■ ALTHOUGH MANY BEGINNING do-it-yourselfers think otherwise, there's no ironclad rule that says an exciting, functional product must be hard to build. The well-designed, easy-to-make projects on these pages prove that's not so. Created from acrylic sheet plastic such as Plexiglas™, they are typical of the gleaming transparent, translucent or opaque household items now so popular in fashionable gift shops and better department stores.

While it looks like glass and comes in sheets like glass, acrylic plastic is as soft as hardwood—

SHEETS of amber Plexiglas were used to make this handsome see-through coffee table, compatible with modern decors.

FISH TANK

CLEAR PLASTIC has many applications. This fish tank is made of it. It can replace glass in doors, for safety, and can be used to make sliding cabinet doors.

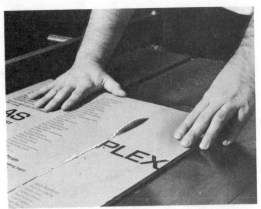

CIRCULAR SAWING: Use a fine-tooth "plywood" blade and set the blade a little higher than the thickness of plastic. Hold material firmly and work slowly.

SABRE SAWING: The blade should have 14 teeth per inch. Use a strip to guide the saw in straight cuts and hold the work firmly on curves.

BANDSAWING: The blade should have a minimum of 10 teeth per inch. Pass the work slowly through the saw. Use protective paper to draw the cutting line.

which means you can drill it and saw it to produce strong transparent joints. You can also heat-form it into interesting curves and shapes—something you can't do with hardwood. The material is widely available from building supply dealers, hardware stores, paint and glass stores, and wallpaper outlets.

Acrylic sheet plastic is made in two forms: safety glazing grade with thicknesses ranging from .080 in. to 3/16 in.; and safety glazing and decorative grade with just two thicknesses, ⅛ in. and ¼ in. The only significant difference between the two is that the safety glazing grade cannot be solvent-cemented.

You can buy sheets in sizes ranging in size from 18 × 24 in. to 36 × 48 in. There are more than 40 standard colors of acrylic plastic from one manufacturer with various tones and eight textured surface patterns.

Although acrylic plastic will scratch more readily than glass, it comes with a protective paper stuck to both sides which is usually left in place while the pieces are being handled and cut.

When working on the projects described on these pages, or one of your own designs, you will want to keep the following in mind:

• **Cutting.** Plastic up to ⅛-in. thick can be cut by scoring and snapping. After it is scored four or five times with a scratch awl, the scored line is centered face up over a ¾-in. dowel. Then the

SCRIBING: Plastic up to ⅛-in. thick can be cut by scoring with a pointed tool. Make the score along a straight-edge, four or five times through the paper.

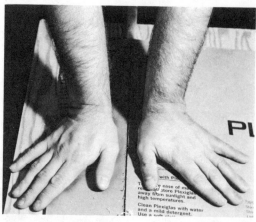

BREAKING: Position the score, face up, directly over a ¾-in. dowel. Hold sheet with one hand and press down with the other. Continue along the score.

DRILLING: Use a regular twist drill and press lightly. Back up the work with a wood block and a clamp. Drill slowly and don't remove the paper.

EDGE FINISHING: Marks are removed by scraping with a knife or by sanding with 60 to 80-grit paper, followed by 150-grit "wet or dry."

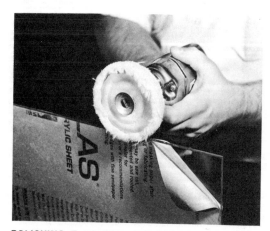

POLISHING: To produce a transparent edge, continue sanding with grits up to 400. Buff with a compound-coated muslin wheel and a cotton-flannel wheel.

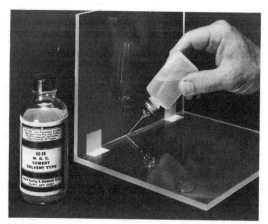

CEMENTING: Remove the paper and sand the surfaces to be cemented. Tape the work and apply solvent to joint with needle-spout unit.

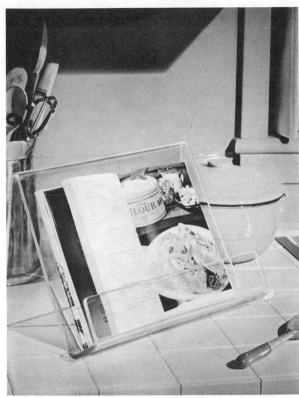

COOKBOOK HOLDER is heat-formed from one piece.

TRISECTED TABLE: Top rests on bent sheets.

TERRARIUM is a good project for beginner.

TELEPHONE STAND requires careful heat-forming.

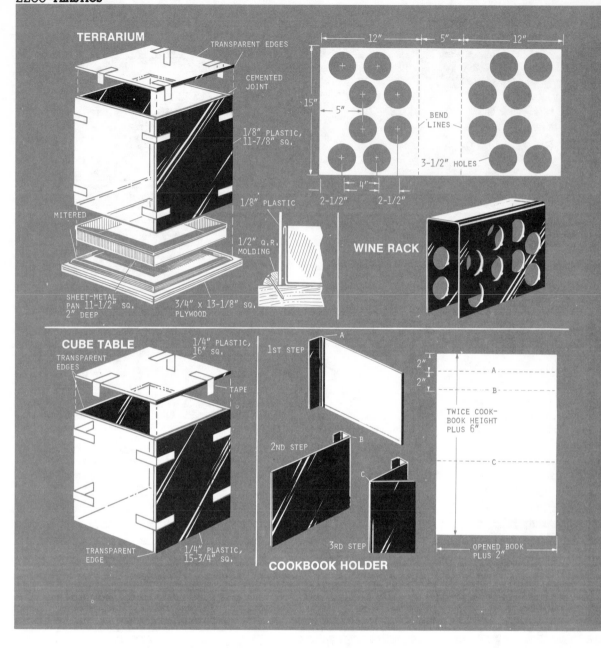

TERRARIUM
- TRANSPARENT EDGES
- CEMENTED JOINT
- 1/8" PLASTIC, 11-7/8" SQ.
- MITERED
- 1/8" PLASTIC
- 1/2" Q.R. MOLDING
- SHEET-METAL PAN 11-1/2" SQ., 2" DEEP
- 3/4" x 13-1/8" SQ., PLYWOOD

- 12"
- 5"
- 12"
- 15"
- 5"
- BEND LINES
- 3-1/2" HOLES
- 4"
- 2-1/2"
- 2-1/2"

WINE RACK

CUBE TABLE
- 1/4" PLASTIC, 16" SQ.
- TRANSPARENT EDGES
- TAPE
- TRANSPARENT EDGE
- 1/4" PLASTIC, 15-3/4" SQ.

COOKBOOK HOLDER
- 1ST STEP — A
- 2ND STEP — B
- 3RD STEP — C
- 2"
- 2"
- A
- B
- TWICE COOK-BOOK HEIGHT PLUS 6"
- C
- OPENED BOOK PLUS 2"

plastic is pressed down on each side to snap it. The minimum snap-off width is about 1½-in. Patterned plastic cannot be scored and broken; it must be sawed.

• **Sawing.** Use either a sabre saw equipped with a fine-tooth blade (32 teeth per inch) or table saw with a plywood-veneer blade. Hold the sheet down firmly and move it slowly through the saw;

do not force. You can also make straight cuts with a special hand tool obtained from the dealer who sold you the plastic.

• **Drilling.** You can use conventional twist drills to bore holes by hand. To do it, back the plastic with a clamped block of wood and be sure the drill is sharp.

To bore with power, use a specially ground

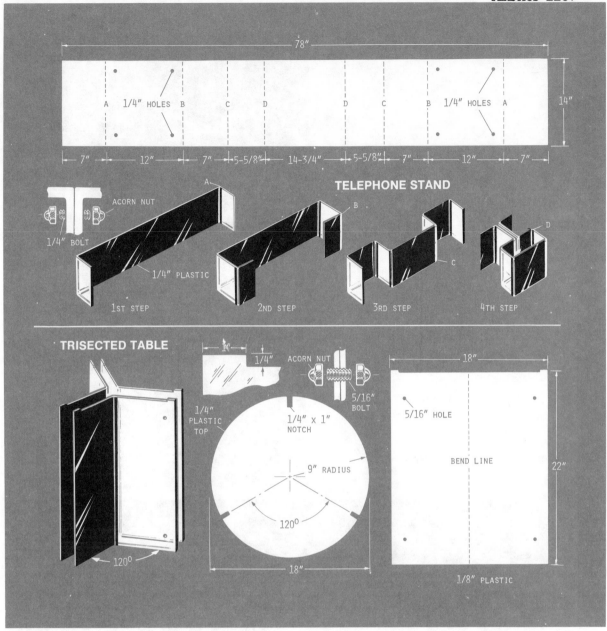

TELEPHONE STAND

78"

14"

A 1/4" HOLES B   C   D   D   C   B 1/4" HOLES A

7" — 12" — 7" — 5-5/8" — 14-3/4" — 5-5/8" — 7" — 12" — 7"

ACORN NUT

1/4" BOLT

A

1/4" PLASTIC

B

C

D

1ST STEP   2ND STEP   3RD STEP   4TH STEP

TRISECTED TABLE

1"

1/4"

ACORN NUT

5/16" BOLT

1/4" PLASTIC TOP

1/4" x 1" NOTCH

9" RADIUS

120°

18"

120°

18"

5/16" HOLE

BEND LINE

22"

1/8" PLASTIC

high-speed twist drill (available from your sheet-plastic dealer). For best results, use a slow speed and minimum pressure: too fast and the plastic will spin with the bit, while too much pressure causes chipping on the back side of the hole.

• **Edge finishing.** Saw and other tool marks should be removed by scraping the edge smooth with a sharp knife or by sanding with a medium-grit (60-80) paper, followed by sanding with "wet or dry" (150) grit paper. For a satin finish, continue to sand with increasingly finer (220-320) wet-or-dry paper. For a transparent finish, sand with finer grit (400-500) wet-or-dry paper and then buff the edges with a clean muslin wheel dressed with a good grade of fine-grit buffing compound. (Note: Buffing kits, with compound, are sold at plastics dealers.)

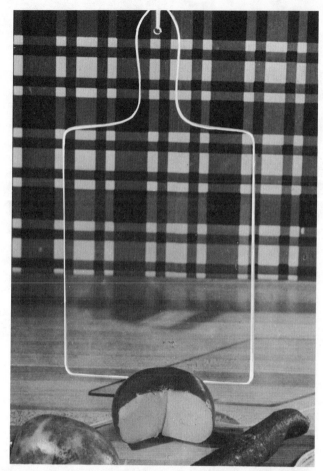

PLASTIC CUTTING BOARD is sanitary, non-absorbent, and is dishwasher-safe. The FDA and the USDA approve clear Plexiglas for such use.

DIAGRAM shows you how to make hat-coat rack shown on the opposite page.

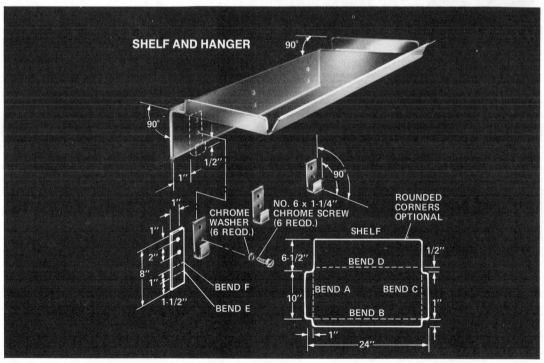

SHELF AND HANGER

90°

90°

1/2''

1''

1''

1''

2''

8''

1''

1-1/2''

CHROME WASHER (6 REQD.)

NO. 6 x 1-1/4'' CHROME SCREW (6 REQD.)

90°

BEND F

BEND E

ROUNDED CORNERS OPTIONAL

SHELF

6-1/2''

BEND D

1/2''

BEND A   BEND C

10''

1''

BEND B

1''

24''

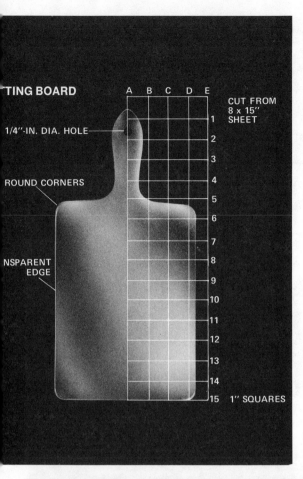

TING BOARD

A B C D E

CUT FROM
8 x 15"
SHEET

1/4"-IN. DIA. HOLE

ROUND CORNERS

NSPARENT
EDGE

1 2 3 4 5 6 7 8 9 10 11 12 13 14 15

1" SQUARES

• **Cementing.** Capillary cementing with a special solvent such as IPS #3 or methylene chloride is an easy and sure way of joining, literally fusing, two pieces of sheet acrylics. First, remove the protective paper from the plastic and sand the edges to a satin finish, as already described. (To save time, bind four panels together and sand the edges simultaneously.) Then place the workpieces together, hold the joint with tabs of masking tape and apply the liquid solvent with a needle-nose applicator made for this purpose (or use an eyedropper, syringe or small paintbrush—not as satisfactory). The liquid will quickly flow into the joint and create an immediate bond. Let it set 20 minutes before removing the tape.

With other types of acrylics, capillary solvent cannot be used. Follow the above directions, except use a thickened cement and clamp the joint for two hours.

Caution: Avoid dripping solvent on the surface of the polished plastic as it will deface it; also work in a well-ventilated room, as solvents may be toxic if inhaled for extended periods. Keep solvents away from flame and children.

• **Bending.** To make a bend, you will need a strip heater, such as the homemade unit shown on these pages that uses a heating element sold by plastics dealers. First, remove the protective paper from the plastic. Then use a grease pencil ("china marker") to mark the plastic where it is to be bent and center the pencil mark over the

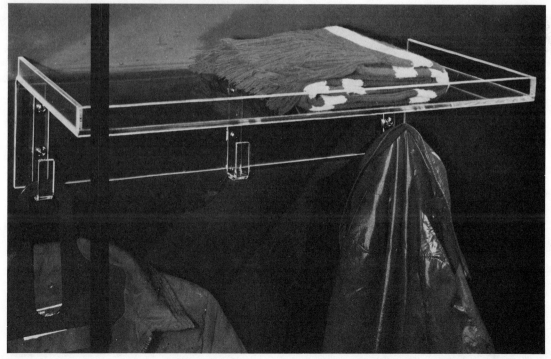

COFFEE TABLE, which stands 16 inches high, is made by combining a favorite wood with a pair of U-shaped legs fashioned of clear plastic. The result is an uncluttered, airy, floating effect.

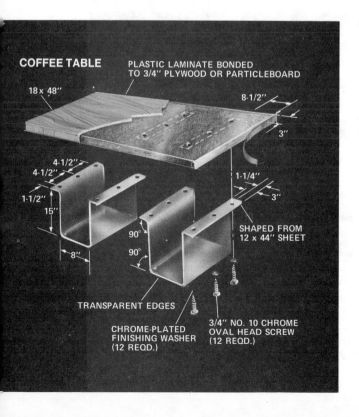

COFFEE TABLE

PLASTIC LAMINATE BONDED TO 3/4" PLYWOOD OR PARTICLEBOARD

18 x 48"

8-1/2"

3"

4-1/2"

4-1/2"

1-1/4"

3"

1-1/2"

15"

90°

SHAPED FROM 12 x 44" SHEET

8"

90°

TRANSPARENT EDGES

CHROME-PLATED FINISHING WASHER (12 REQD.)

3/4" NO. 10 CHROME OVAL HEAD SCREW (12 REQD.)

heater element. It will take from 8 to 10 min. at the desired temperature of about 290°F to heat ¼-in.-thick plastic to a bendable state. Make the bend slowly, on the line, while the plastic is still on the heater. You'll find that the plastic has a tendency to "spring" back as it cools, so you must compensate a bit when forming a right-angle bend. Hold the bent material until the softened plastic cools and hardens.

Be careful not to overheat the plastic; it will scorch and bubble if you do. Bending it before it is soft enough will cause stress crazing (small internal fractures) at the bend. Practice on a scrap first. The temperature of the plastic should not be greater than 340°F., and don't try to bend plastic more than ¼-in. thick with the heater. In any event, *do not* heat sheet acrylic in your oven; doing so could cause an explosion.

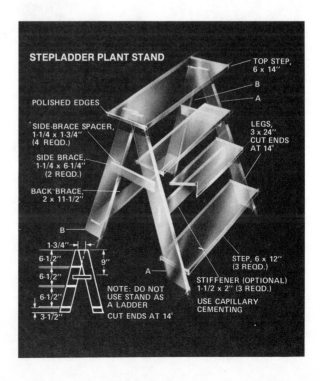

STEPLADDER PLANT STAND

TOP STEP,
6 x 14"

B

A

POLISHED EDGES

SIDE-BRACE SPACER,
1-1/4 x 1-3/4"
(4 REQD.)

LEGS,
3 x 24"
CUT ENDS
AT 14°

SIDE BRACE,
1-1/4 x 6-1/4"
(2 REQD.)

BACK BRACE,
2 x 11-1/2"

B

1-3/4"
6-1/2"
9"
6-1/2"
6-1/2"
3-1/2"

A

STEP, 6 x 12"
(3 REQD.)

STIFFENER (OPTIONAL)
1-1/2 x 2" (3 REQD.)

NOTE: DO NOT
USE STAND AS
A LADDER

CUT ENDS AT 14°

USE CAPILLARY
CEMENTING

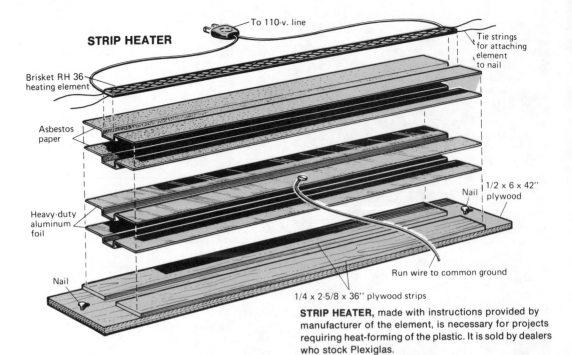

To 110-v. line

STRIP HEATER

Tie strings for attaching element to nail

Brisket RH 36 heating element

Asbestos paper

Heavy-duty aluminum foil

Nail

1/2 x 6 x 42'' plywood

Run wire to common ground

Nail

1/4 x 2-5/8 x 36'' plywood strips

STRIP HEATER, made with instructions provided by manufacturer of the element, is necessary for projects requiring heat-forming of the plastic. It is sold by dealers who stock Plexiglas.

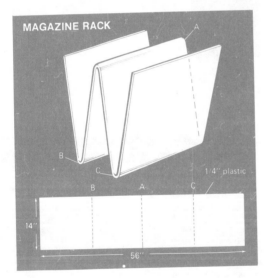

MAGAZINE RACK

A

B

C

1/4'' plastic

B   A   C

14''

56''

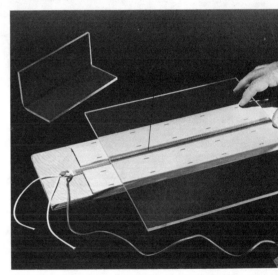

TO BEND PLASTIC, protective paper is removed and plastic is placed over heat tape in strip heater.

Internal carving: a little-known art

■ ACCORDING TO EXPERTS in the acrylic plastic field, internal carving was the first popular plastics craft. The fine optical characteristics of clear plastic not only make this art possible, but enable you to create effects that are impossible with any other carving technique.

The biggest delight for most internal carvers, after they have acquired the necessary skills, is to produce objects which are edge-lit. The Lincoln head, for example, when mounted on a wood base containing a 7-w. bulb, produces a striking three-dimensional look when the bulb is lighted. The reason: the light passes through the uncarved area and is not visible to the eye. But, the carved-out portion will reflect every mark that you've made with your cutters.

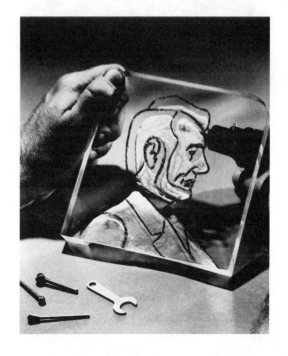

A fine tool for small carving projects is a hobbyist's motor tool. It was used to carve all the projects you see on these pages. With a foot rheostat, the tool performed well on light chores. Though it did require some cooling-off periods when large areas were being ground out, the tool did all that the maker claims it will when restricted to the hobbyist-type chores for which it is intended.

If you're a beginner, you should start with simple designs which will keep you pretty much confined to using round or barrel-type cutters. Don't be disappointed if your first few tries don't even resemble the design you've drawn on the face. It takes practice and more practice to learn the nuances and tricks that the art demands. But once you've mastered the tools of the trade, you'll be more than pleased with what you can turn out.

To carve, hold the piece of plastic between thumb and forefinger of one hand, and the carving tool in your other hand with the drill bit facing up to the bottom of the plastic. As you carve, you will look down into the work. With a round burr, form a cavity in the underside. Don't hurry the job and do let the drill do the work. A good project to start with is a simple shape such as your house number or initials. After a while you'll automatically manipulate the drill expertly enough to take on such sophisticated projects as flowers, birds and fish.

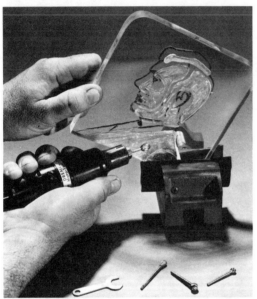

BACK VIEW of carving shows varying depths of cut. When the carving is finished, a colored sheet plastic (right) is affixed to it by means of double-faced tape. If desired, the carving can be painted.

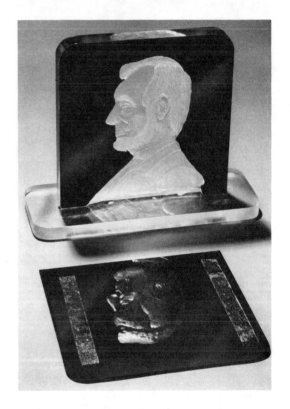

Playground play structures

■ DESIGN OUTDOOR PLAY equipment that's fun for kids, yet visually appealing to adults. That was the challenge given to an architect; returned with several ingenious creations. Two with modifications are shown here for you to duplicate.

Materials and construction notes

For durability, use pressure-treated lumber. Select wood that carries the American Wood Preservers Bureau (AWPB) quality seal, is labeled "CCA" (chromated copper arsenate) or with another waterborne preservative and is dry after treatment so the preservative won't leach out of the wood. Posts and lumber that contact the soil should be labeled "LP-22 ground contact .40" Select No. 1 grade wood to minimize splintering. In addition, ease all edges and chamfer or round ends.

Use hot-dipped, galvanized or cadmium-plated hardware. In most situations, carriage bolts are recommended, pounded into prebored holes to admit the shoulders and secured with countersunk washers and nuts tightened from the back.

First, counterbore the nut hole, then clamp the two members together and bore through them. If the bolt ends protrude, mark, remove and cut them flush with a hacksaw.

Planning the play site

Carefully planning your child's outdoor play site will greatly reduce the chance of accidents.

Select a level space. Consider the location of underground power lines, sprinkler systems, water and telephone lines. To avoid placing a slide or swing too near a tree, for example, it helps to make a scaled diagram of the area with the proposed equipment. You'll also be able to plan an adequate safety apron, the ground around the equipment, which should be topped with semisoft material.

Border the play areas with sunken railroad ties "a safe distance" from the equipment. On equipment 4 ft. high, this means 4 to 5 ft. in all directions. The border for a swing suspended from a 10-ft.-high bar should be 10 ft. in front and back. After installation, fill the play area with bark or

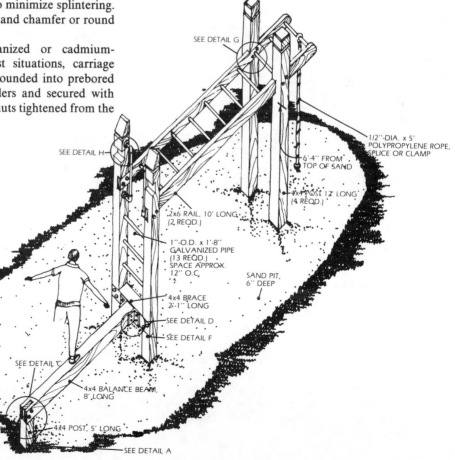

SEE DETAIL G

SEE DETAIL H

1/2"-DIA. x 5'
POLYPROPYLENE ROPE,
SPLICE OR CLAMP

6'-4" FROM
TOP OF SAND

4x4 POST 12' LONG
(4 REQD.)

2x6 RAIL, 10' LONG
(2 REQD.)

1"-O.D. x 1'-8"
GALVANIZED PIPE
(13 REQD.)
SPACE APPROX.
12" O.C.

SAND PIT,
6" DEEP

4x4 BRACE
2'-1" LONG

SEE DETAIL D

SEE DETAIL F

SEE DETAIL C

4x4 BALANCE BEAM,
8' LONG

4x4 POST, 5' LONG

SEE DETAIL A

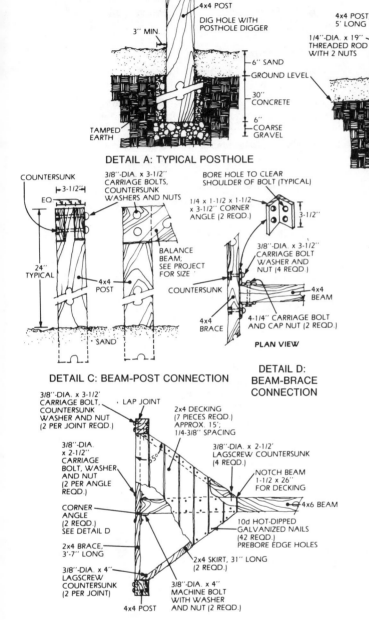

3" MIN.

4x4 POST

DIG HOLE WITH POSTHOLE DIGGER

6" SAND
GROUND LEVEL
30" CONCRETE
6" COARSE GRAVEL

TAMPED EARTH

DETAIL A: TYPICAL POSTHOLE

COUNTERSUNK

3/8"-DIA. x 3-1/2" CARRIAGE BOLTS, COUNTERSUNK WASHERS AND NUTS

BORE HOLE TO CLEAR SHOULDER OF BOLT (TYPICAL)

1/4 x 1-1/2 x 1-1/2 x 3-1/2" CORNER ANGLE (2 REQD.)

3-1/2"

EQ.

24" TYPICAL

4x4 POST

BALANCE BEAM; SEE PROJECT FOR SIZE

COUNTERSUNK

4x4 BRACE

3/8"-DIA. x 3-1/2" CARRIAGE BOLT WASHER AND NUT (4 REQD.)

4x4 BEAM

4-1/4" CARRIAGE BOLT AND CAP NUT (2 REQD.)

SAND

PLAN VIEW

DETAIL C: BEAM-POST CONNECTION

DETAIL D: BEAM-BRACE CONNECTION

3/8"-DIA. x 3-1/2" CARRIAGE BOLT, COUNTERSUNK WASHER AND NUT (2 PER JOINT REQD.)

LAP JOINT

3/8"-DIA. x 2-1/2" CARRIAGE BOLT, WASHER AND NUT (2 PER ANGLE REQD.)

CORNER ANGLE (2 REQD.) SEE DETAIL D

2x4 BRACE, 3'-7" LONG

3/8"-DIA. x 4" LAGSCREW COUNTERSUNK (2 PER JOINT)

2x4 DECKING (7 PIECES REQD.) APPROX. 15'; 1/4-3/8" SPACING

3/8"-DIA. x 2-1/2" LAGSCREW COUNTERSUNK (4 REQD.)

NOTCH BEAM 1-1/2 x 26" FOR DECKING

4x6 BEAM

10d HOT-DIPPED GALVANIZED NAILS (42 REQD.) PREBORE EDGE HOLES

2x4 SKIRT, 31" LONG (2 REQD.)

4x4 POST

3/8"-DIA. x 4" MACHINE BOLT WITH WASHER AND NUT (2 REQD.)

DETAIL E: PLATFORM, PLAN VIEW

4x4, 4'-6" LONG, (2 REQD.); BURY 2'-6" INTO GROUND

4x4 POST, 5' LONG

1/4"-DIA. x 19" THREADED ROD WITH 2 NUTS

1/4"-DIA. x 9-1/2" THREADED ROD WITH 2 NUTS

1"-DIA. HOLE x 1"-DEEP COUNTERBORE (TYPICAL)

4x4, 4' LONG (2 REQD.); BURY 2'-6" INTO GROUND

DETAIL B: BALANCE STEPS

Installing outdoor equipment

Heavy wood equipment requires solid anchoring. There are three major concerns in determining adequate anchors: the *stress* to the equipment, the *soil* in which the equipment (posts) is installed and the *frost line* in your area.

A swing set that undergoes torque movement, for example, should be anchored deeper than a slide that doesn't receive this type of stress. A concrete collar in sandy soil should be deeper and wider than a collar in clay soil. Generally, wooden posts for home play equipment are installed 18 to 24 in. deep or to the frost line. Your local building codes can tell you the depth of the frost line in your area.

Maintaining play equipment

Following is a checklist of spring maintenance tips from the Consumer Product Safety Commission: Clear away debris, roots and rocks; tighten loose nuts, bolts and clamps; oil moving metal parts; sand rusted areas and paint with unleaded paint; replace rusted chains; cap or plug exposed ends of tubing; close S-hooks, rings and links; refill landing pits with sand or bark; and sand splintered areas.

Project 1: beam and pole

This project incorporates a fireman's pole. The pole top is held in a tee-fitting, to which two sections of pipe curved 90° are also fastened (see detail I).

An electrical contractor with an electric or hydraulic bender can curve sections of pipe cut to size and threaded at the ends. You might be able to create the curved top of the pole with sections of straight pipe and cast 90° elbows.

The drawing gives dimensions of the wood parts. Details A, B, D, E and I give fastener tips.

pine straw to a 6-in. depth. Sand is also good. Trees and bushes should be left nearby for shade.

All outdoor play equipment should have installation instructions made specifically for the equipment. It is important to follow these instructions.

Begin by cutting the steps (detail B) and posts (detail A) of 4 x 4s. Cut the 2 x 4 brace. Ease all edges, including those on the beam, and make decorative cuts and kerfs. Bore 1½-in.-deep holes for the chinning bar and cut notches for the brace connection on the two major posts. Notch the beam for the decking.

Mark and cut the post that connects to the beam (detail C) with a dado blade on a radial-arm saw. Set the blade to cut a 1⅛-in. depth and cut the post on both sides. Mark the notch to be cut on the beam and bore out both corners of the notch. Cut out the notch with a hand saw and use a sharp chisel to clear out waste.

Set the beam on the post and clamp or tack-nail it; counterbore for the washers and nuts. Then bore through-holes for the carriage bolts. Don't assemble the parts yet.

Counterbore holes in the short post (at the other end) and steps for nuts that hold connecting rods (detail B). Bore holes for the attachment rods. Join the steps with the rods and nuts. Secure the beam to the short post.

Install the chinning bar and platform brace (detail E) on the major posts. Secure the beam to the brace with a corner angle cut to size.

At this point, test-position the assembly. Then dig postholes (detail A) with a clamshell posthole digger. You can use a shovel to dig holes for the steps. Pour gravel into the holes. Position the structure and rock it slightly to seat it on the gravel. Plumb and level, brace if needed, and pour concrete collars.

Next, install the deck skirts and the rough-cut deck members with ¼- to ⅜-in. spaces between them. After installation, snap a chalkline and trim with a combination blade in a circular saw so it just cuts through the decking.

Thread the tee-fitting on to the fireman's pole (detail I). Thread both pipe quadrants onto the tee and into flanges on the other ends. Test-position the pole and dig its hole with a clamshell posthole digger. Install the pole; tamp the backfilled earth. Secure the flanges to the posts. Finally, add 6 in. of sand around the area.

Project 2: beam and ladder

A number of children can enjoy this design at the same time. The drawing gives dimensions of the wood parts. Details A, C, D, F, G and H give fastening information.

Cut the posts, balance beam, rails and braces to size if needed. Ease the edges and round or chamfer the ends. Make decorative kerfs and cuts in the posts. Cut notches in the posts for the rails

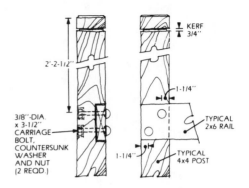

DETAIL G: POST-RAIL CONNECTION

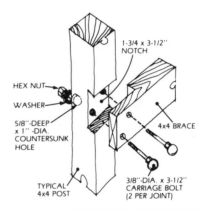

DETAIL F: POST-BRACE CONNECTION

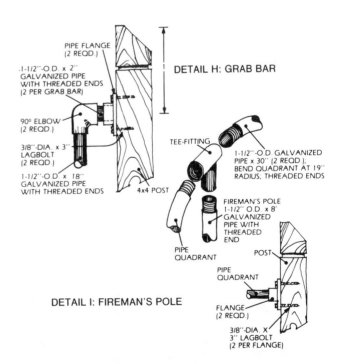

DETAIL H: GRAB BAR

DETAIL I: FIREMAN'S POLE

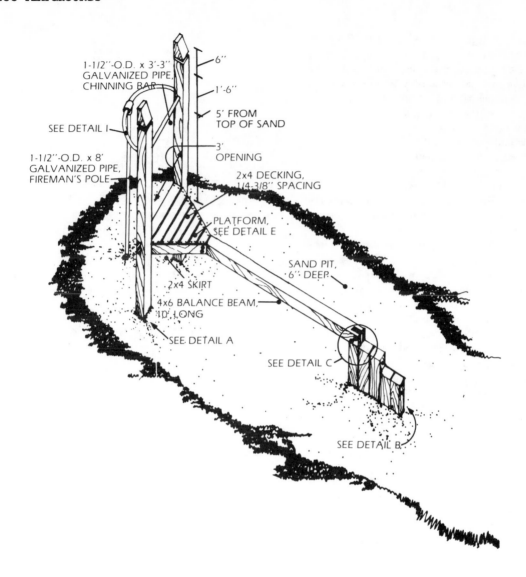

1-1/2″-O.D. x 3′-3″ GALVANIZED PIPE, CHINNING BAR

6″

1′-6″

5′ FROM TOP OF SAND

SEE DETAIL I

3′ OPENING

1-1/2″-O.D. x 8′ GALVANIZED PIPE, FIREMAN'S POLE

2x4 DECKING, 1/4-3/8″ SPACING

PLATFORM, SEE DETAIL E

SAND PIT, 6″ DEEP

2x4 SKIRT

4x6 BALANCE BEAM, 10′ LONG

SEE DETAIL A

SEE DETAIL C

SEE DETAIL B

(detail G) and brace (detail F). Carefully mark aligned holes for the pipe bars in the rails and posts; bore holes 1 in. deep.

Mark and cut the post that connects to the beam (detail C) and notch the beam (see explanation for making this joint in Project No. 1). Secure the pieces.

Install the pipe bars in the rails and temporarily tack crossbraces on both ends to keep the rails together. Next, install pipe bars in the posts. Temporarily tack a crossbrace near the top pipe and secure the brace that connects to the beam (detail F).

Install the rail assembly onto the posts (detail G), leaving a 7-ft., 8½-in. space between posts. The rail assembly will extend 1 ft., 8½ in. beyond the posts at one end. Join the balance beam to its brace with two corner angles (detail D).

Dig postholes for the footings with a clamshell posthole digger (detail A). Pour gravel into the holes and position the unit, rocking the posts to seat them on the gravel. Plumb and level; brace if needed. Pour in concrete.

Install grab bars (detail H) and secure the polypropylene rope. The rope, which is meant for climbing, can be anchored at the free end or omitted for safety if the play area isn't supervised. Fill the area with 6 in. of sand.

Playground fun

Merry-go-round swing

WHEN YOU LAY out the location for this toy, allow plenty of room so the kids can swing and twist on it in all directions. For a base, cut a 3-ft. disc from ¾-in. exterior plywood. Bore four holes equidistant around the circumference 2 in. from the edge. Secure with short hemp ropes knotted below and fasten to a length of rope attached to an overhead horizontal crosspiece between two trees.

Bouncing teeter board

IT'S POSSIBLE to add playground equipment to your back-yard "family-fun center" without spending a great deal of money. With a little imagination, you can convert everyday items that no longer serve their original purpose into games for your youngsters. The teeter board, for example, is simply four coil springs from a car attached to an old wheel hub. Use a heavy truck tire for a base and a 2x10 plank for the board. Paint in bright colors.

Backyard summer fun

YOUR CHILDREN are sure to enjoy the swing and stilts shown as much as the children in these photos are. Both projects have been made of durable hardwood for years of heavy, outdoor use.

■ YOUNGSTERS LIKE ALL KINDS of presents from the most complicated and expensive to the simplest and cheapest. But they're happiest when they know that you made the present yourself. The four games on these pages are easy to build, and one of them will suit your boy or girl (and some grownups if they get a chance to play), no matter what their age. You won't need any special tools to construct the stilts, swing, tetherball or basketball hoop. Since these games are played outdoors, you have to build them to withstand the weather. Make the swing out of solid oak stock and protect the pieces with two coats of spar varnish. All wood joints should be assembled with a waterproof glue or construction adhesive and all nails should be hot-dipped galvanized to prevent rust. For screws, use brass or aluminum.

The most complicated project, the basketball hoop, is worth the effort because the backstop adjusts to any height. The detail drawing (next page) shows how the heavy plywood backstop weights down the upper frame to get a clamping action between cross ties and 4x4 support posts. The cam action is so tight that 2x4 chocks under the cross ties on opposite sides of the posts will support the whole assembly. This system lets you raise the hoop as your children get taller.

A pair of stilts is a great toy to develop balance and coordination. Use a hardwood like oak or maple for the stock and base pad. Exterior-grade plywood is fine for the foot platform that will easily support a 75-lb. child. For larger children, add the alternate brace detailed in the drawings. To preserve the stilts and prevent scrapes and bruises to a minimum, tell the children to stay off hard surfaces.

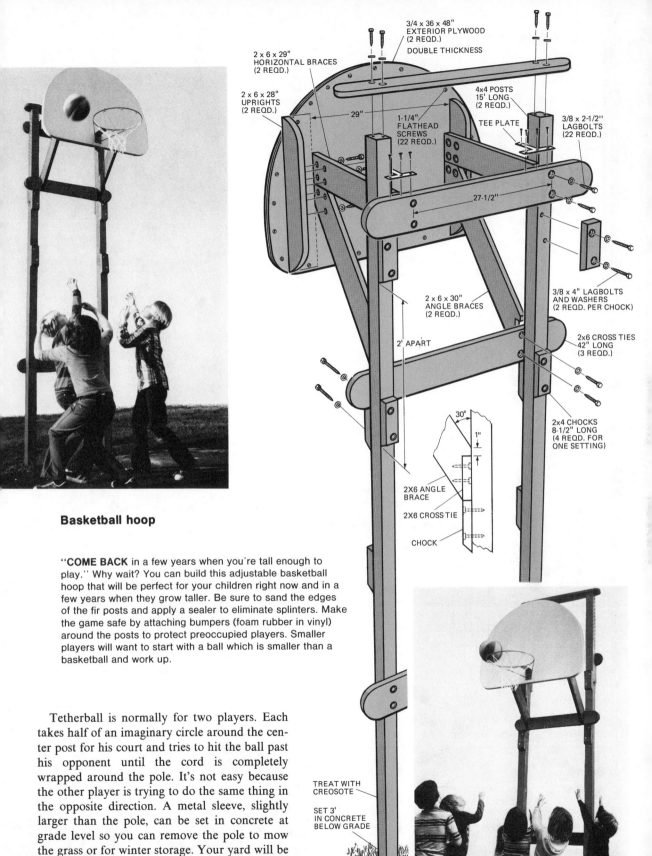

3/4 x 36 x 48"
EXTERIOR PLYWOOD
(2 REQD.)
DOUBLE THICKNESS

2 x 6 x 29"
HORIZONTAL BRACES
(2 REQD.)

2 x 6 x 28"
UPRIGHTS
(2 REQD.)

4x4 POSTS
15' LONG
(2 REQD.)

29"

1-1/4"
FLATHEAD
SCREWS
(22 REQD.)

TEE PLATE

3/8 x 2-1/2"
LAGBOLTS
(22 REQD.)

27-1/2"

2 x 6 x 30"
ANGLE BRACES
(2 REQD.)

3/8 x 4" LAGBOLTS
AND WASHERS
(2 REQD. PER CHOCK)

2' APART

2x6 CROSS TIES
42" LONG
(3 REQD.)

30°

1"

2X6 ANGLE
BRACE

2X6 CROSS TIE

CHOCK

2x4 CHOCKS
8-1/2" LONG
(4 REQD. FOR
ONE SETTING)

TREAT WITH
CREOSOTE

SET 3'
IN CONCRETE
BELOW GRADE

Basketball hoop

"**COME BACK** in a few years when you're tall enough to play." Why wait? You can build this adjustable basketball hoop that will be perfect for your children right now and in a few years when they grow taller. Be sure to sand the edges of the fir posts and apply a sealer to eliminate splinters. Make the game safe by attaching bumpers (foam rubber in vinyl) around the posts to protect preoccupied players. Smaller players will want to start with a ball which is smaller than a basketball and work up.

Tetherball is normally for two players. Each takes half of an imaginary circle around the center post for his court and tries to hit the ball past his opponent until the cord is completely wrapped around the pole. It's not easy because the other player is trying to do the same thing in the opposite direction. A metal sleeve, slightly larger than the pole, can be set in concrete at grade level so you can remove the pole to mow the grass or for winter storage. Your yard will be a special place for the children after you've built one of these toys.

Child's swing

WHATEVER the object, a child will try to swing from it if it's possible. This good-looking design, assembled around a continuous rope loop, eliminates screwed joints that may split open under stress. The guard rails lift up along the ropes for easy access (you can face in either direction) and slide down to make an accidental fall next to impossible. Use nylon rope for a safer ride

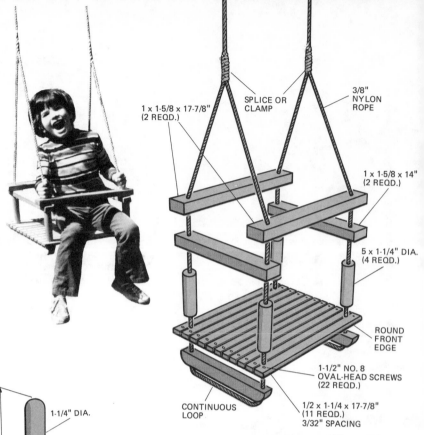

SPLICE OR CLAMP

3/8" NYLON ROPE

1 x 1-5/8 x 17-7/8" (2 REQD.)

1 x 1-5/8 x 14" (2 REQD.)

5 x 1-1/4" DIA. (4 REQD.)

ROUND FRONT EDGE

1-1/2" NO. 8 OVAL-HEAD SCREWS (22 REQD.)

1/2 x 1-1/4 x 17-7/8" (11 REQD.) 3/32" SPACING

CONTINUOUS LOOP

Stilts

WE TESTED this design, and the foot platform held up after rough use by a 150-pounder. To play safe, use the alternate brace for anyone over 75 lbs. This pair is sealed with clear varnish, but you can decorate yours with bright enamel colors or contrasting wood stains

1-1/4" HOLE X 2-1/2" DEEP

1-1/4" DIA.

3/4"   1/4"

2"

2 1/2"

1/4"

ALTERNATE BRACE

46-1/2" LONG

2 1/2" NO.8 SCREW (2 REQD.)

2" NO. 8 BRASS FLAT-HEAD SCREW

1-7/8 x 1-7/8 x 16" HARDWOOD

4-3/8"

7/8 x 3/4" GROOVE

4-3/4"

3/4" EXTERIOR PLYWOOD

PAD

3-1/8"   2-9/16"

3/4" COUNTERSINK 3/8" DRILL

Tetherball

THE TOUGHEST part of this project is locating a ball with a moulded loop on it. A 6-in.-diameter, concrete filled hole makes a strong, permanent base. Setting an oversize sleeve in the concrete will make the pole demountable. Tetherball is a game the whole family will enjoy

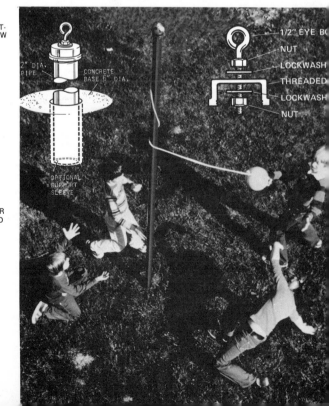

1/2" EYE BO

NUT

LOCKWASH

THREADED

LOCKWASH

NUT

2" DIA. PIPE

CONCRETE BASE 6" DIA.

OPTIONAL SUPPORT SLEEVE

Super sandbox you can build

■ YOUNGSTERS WILL PLAY by the hour in this inviting sandbox. When the children are grown, it can be closed in to serve as a utility shed.

The sandbox is made using 2x4 framing covered with weather-resistant cedar siding. It features a redwood seat and hip-roof construction. Use pressure-treated wood for the framing, rails and posts.

Prepare the ground for the sandbox. First mark out the 4x4-ft. sandbox area using stakes and a mason's line and check each corner of the rectangle to be sure it is square.

Level the area to a 6-in. depth. Then set the corner posts below the frost line and chamfer the inside edges.

Add a 4-in.-deep gravel layer and top it with 1 or 2 in. of mason's sand. Rake the sand level and tamp. Lay the brick floor.

Begin work on the sandbox section. Corner members Y are 2x4s notched to receive the rails.

The framing of the sandbox entry is somewhat tricky. To avoid having to drive nails through a full 2x4 width, notch the bottom plate to receive the filler strip.

Next, cut a 1½x1¾x19-in. strip from a scrap 2x4. Secure the notched legs X by spiking with nails. Then nail-fasten the strip into the notch cut in the bottom plate. Use 10d common nails and drill pilot holes to avoid splitting. Assemble the other three sides using resorcinol glue and nails. Attach the sides to the corner posts.

Before installing the cedar siding, bevel all edges using either a router or table saw. The flat next to the bevel should be at least ⅝-in. wide to assure adequate material meeting at the joints.

Install the siding, one board at a time, in this fashion:

1 Make a 45° miter cut on one end; hold the board in position on the frame, mitered end at the bottom of the sandbox.

2 Mark the miter cut at the upper end, remove board and make cut.

3 Install the siding using resorcinol glue and 6d galvanized nails. Sink nails and fill holes.

For durability, build the sandbox seat of either redwood or pressure-treated wood. Use miter cuts at the corner joints to give a professional look to the job. Notch the corners where they meet the posts.

Center the seat on the 2x4 frame and attach it with resorcinol glue and 6d galvanized finishing nails. Set the nails and cover them with a weatherproof wood filler.

The roof is a square hip roof with a 6½-in. pitch (6½-in. rise in a 12-in. run). Construction is of 2x4 framing skinned with ½-in. plywood sheathing.

Cut the 2 x 4 frame parts and 1 x 2 ceiling cleats. Predrill holes and attach frame to posts using No. 18 3½-in. lagscrews.

Cut the ceiling, make corner notches for the posts, and attach to the ceiling cleats. Roof rafters rest on the corner posts. Install rafters with No. 18 3½-in. lagscrews. Nail the sheathing to the roof with 8d common nails.

SUPER SANDBOX

2 x 4 RAFTER
(4 REQD.)

1 x 6 ROUGH CEDAR FASCIA

44-3/4" O.A.

60"

45-1/2" O.A.

45"

4 x 4 POST
(4 REQD.)

45"

2 x 4 FRAMING

60"

PLAN OF ROOF FRAMING

15-LB. FELT

ASPHALT SHINGLES
(4 BUNDLES REQUIRED)

37-3/4"

STARTER COURSE
(SHINGLES REVERSED)

1/2" CDX PLYWOOD
(4 REQD.)

ADD SCREENING OR SOFFIT WITH VENTS TO KEEP NEST-BUILDING INSECTS OUT

2 x 4

3/4 x 1-1/2 x 33"
(4 REQD.)

2 x 2"
INSECT SCREEN

3/4"
PLYWOOD

3/4" DIA.
VENT HOLE
(4 PLACES)

1 x 6 FASCIA

4 x 4 POST

CEILING DETAIL

7-1/4"

3-5/8" 3-5/8"

2 x 4 FRAMING

SEAT TOP,
1 x 8 REDWOOD

1 x 4 ROUGH CEDAR ON 45° ANGLE

19-1/2"

PLYWOOD CEILING,
3/4 x 45 x 45"

4 x 4 POSTS
6' HIGH

1 x 6 ROUGH SAWN CEDAR FASCIA

1-3/4" 1-3/4"

3-1/2"

6-1/2"

3"

DETAIL X

3-1/2"

CUT FROM 2 x 4's

3-1/2"

3"

DETAIL Y

3"

10"

3-1/2"

1-3/4"

3-1/2 x 7-1/2"
BRICKS,
(100 REQD.)

3-1/2" 3-1/2"

38"

1-1/2" 3-1/2"   3-1/2" 1-1/2"

3-1/2"

3-1/2"

14-1/2"   12"   14-1/2"
1-3/4"   1-3/4"   1-3/4"

3-1/2"
2 x 4   1-3/4"   2 x 4

10"
Y   X   X   Y

2 x 4

19"

ENTRANCE RAIL

SEE DETAILS

PLAN VIEW

4 x 4 POST,
6' HIGH
(4 REQD.)

38"

3-1/2"

3-1/2"
2 x 4
3"
Y   Y
3-1/2"
2 x 4

TYPICAL SIDE AND REAR RAILS

MAKE REAR RAIL 48" LONG,
SIDE RAILS 45" LONG

3-1/2"

A-frame swing set

■ USING AN A-FRAME for strength, this swing set is very stable. If you can find some materials at the junkyard it will cost less.

Choose a 16 x 18-ft. site for the swing set. It should be fairly level and clear of shrubs and other obstacles. In addition, the sliding board will extend about 12 ft. from one side. Level four block footings before starting on the A-frame.

To construct the frame, assemble the two A-shaped sides on the ground. Use temporary gussets at the vertex and bolts at other intersections.

Raise, position and plumb each preassembled side with the aid of a helper. Use 1 x 2 furring as temporary braces until you can nail on the floor joists, ridge board and plywood floor. Temporary braces extending from the front (pole side) and rear (slide side) to ground stakes should remain until the roof sheathing is in place. Frame the swing set as shown in the plans.

Note that swing-support headers are pinned to header joists. Bore ⅜-in.-dia. holes in these joists and insert ⅜-in.-dia. steel rod. Bore mating holes in the support header and slip it over the pins. Heavy-duty 5-in. corner braces can also be used in place of pins.

The foot of the slide must be securely anchored to a concrete base, since this will prevent the A-frame from swaying. Prepare a form and locate anchor bolts for securing the slide to the base plate. After the concrete has been poured and allowed to set, the slide rails can be attached. Notice that the rails are built in three sections. Use ⅜-in.-dia. x 3-in. carriage bolts to join them together and counterbore so threaded ends of bolts don't snag children.

Secure the top end of the rails to the 2 x 4 loft joists. Use a mending plate and No. 10 rh screws or bolts. Fasten the rails to the slide base plate after it has been secured to the anchor bolts in the concrete.

Next, build the bottom end of the slide. The underside of the lower rail boards are curved at one end. Use the lid of a 20-gal. trash can to mark the arc before cutting.

Now attach the galvanized sheet metal to the underside of the slide rails. Use ¼-in.-dia. x 1½-in. lagscrews with washers. The metal edges should be recessed about ¾ in. from the rails' outer edges. Leave enough extra metal at top and bottom so it can be wrapped under the cross members and then fastened securely with more lagscrews.

On the opposite side of the A-frame install the fireman's pole. Sink it at least 1 ft. into the ground or into a concrete footing. Attach the top to the ridgeboard with metal strapping. Other accessories, as shown in the plans, can be added at your discretion. Use ⅜-in. nylon rope or chain to hang the various ladders, swings and trapezes.

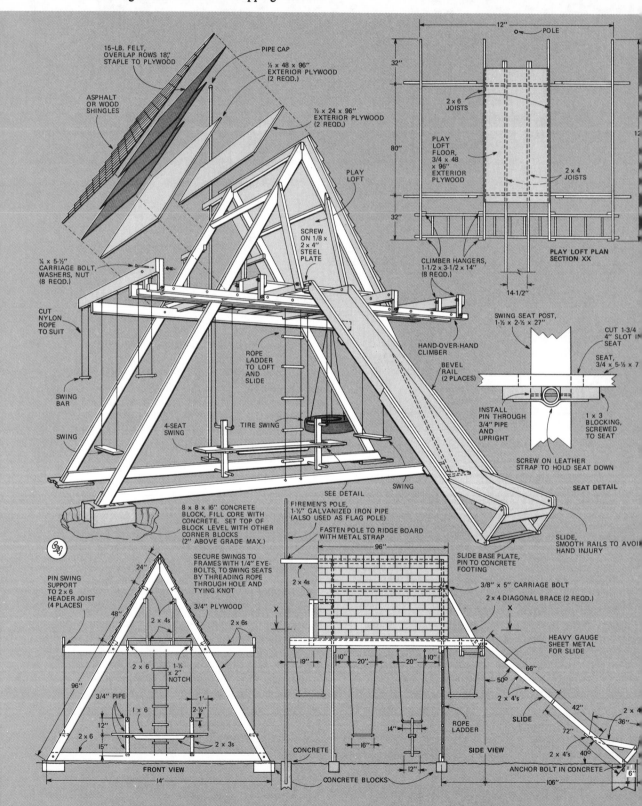

Play tower you can build with a chain saw

■ THERE CAN BE little doubt that many chain-saw owners bought their tools for no other task than cutting firewood. It's true that a small but powerful chain saw makes relatively quick and easy work of cutting up a cord of firewood. But the tool can also be used for many project-building tasks.

You can create an attractive, useful project that could be built using very few tools besides the chain saw.

The challenge we gave our designer was to come up with a functional backyard play structure, built of sturdy members to assure a long life. A master craftsman took the designer's sketch and created the structure shown, working out all construction details as he went. The result is the easy-to-follow plans on the following pages.

The basic structure is made of 2x4, 2x6 and 4x4

ROOF IS covered with handsome cedar shakes. It has a wide overhang to provide shelter from showers.

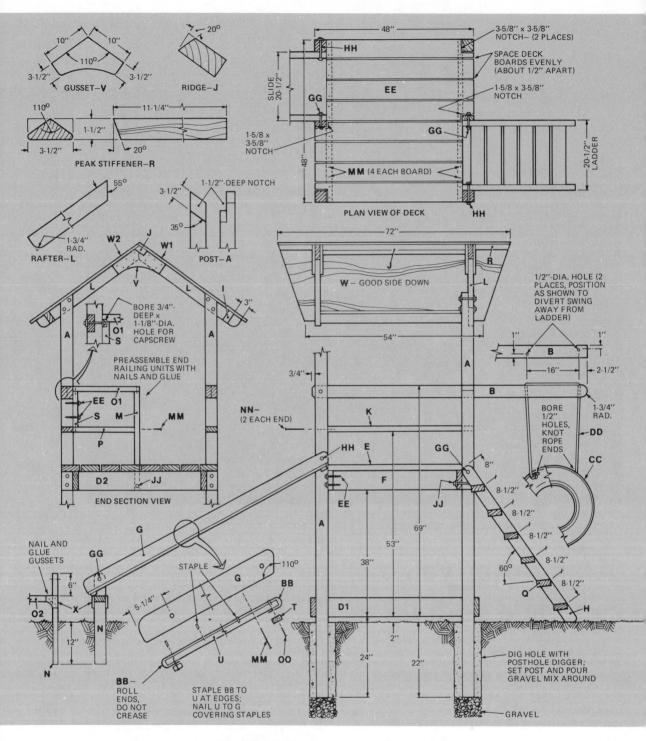

pressure-treated stock. (The actual measurements are given in the materials list.) We recommend that you use pressure-treated stock (Wolmanized was used in the structure shown) where members are in contact with the soil, because this lumber is both water- and insect-resistant. If you prefer, use cedar posts and conventional fir 2x4s and 2x6s. To prevent rotting, apply at least three coats of a wood preservative.

Chain-saw joinery

Before starting, make certain that the chain is

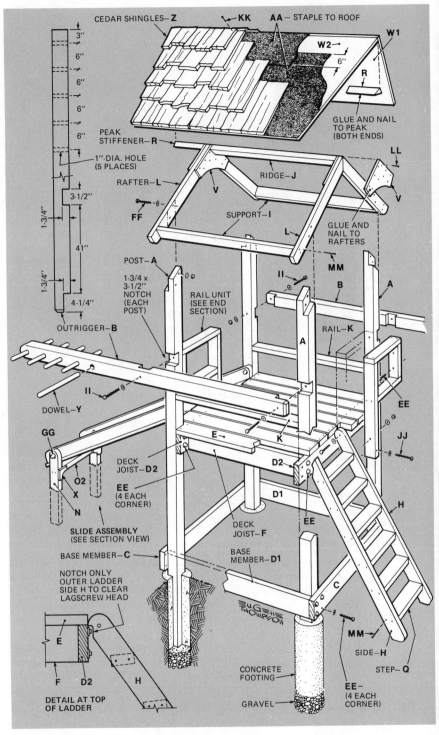

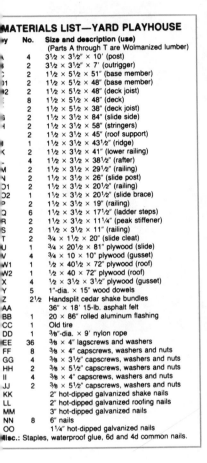

MATERIALS LIST—YARD PLAYHOUSE

Key	No.	Size and description (use)
		(Parts A through T are Wolmanized lumber)
A	4	3½ × 3½ × 10′ (post)
B	2	3½ × 3½ × 7′ (outrigger)
C	2	1½ × 5½ × 51″ (base member)
D1	2	1½ × 5½ × 48″ (base member)
D2	2	1½ × 5½ × 48″ (deck joist)
E	8	1½ × 5½ × 48″ (deck)
F	2	1½ × 5½ × 38″ (deck joist)
G	2	1½ × 3½ × 84″ (slide side)
H	2	1½ × 3½ × 58″ (stringers)
I	2	1½ × 3½ × 45″ (roof support)
J	1	1½ × 3½ × 43½″ (ridge)
K	2	1½ × 3½ × 41″ (lower railing)
L	4	1½ × 3½ × 38½″ (rafter)
M	2	1½ × 3½ × 29½″ (railing)
N	2	1½ × 3½ × 26″ (slide post)
O1	2	1½ × 3½ × 20½″ (railing)
O2	1	1½ × 3½ × 20½″ (slide brace)
P	2	1½ × 3½ × 19″ (railing)
Q	6	1½ × 3½ × 17½″ (ladder steps)
R	2	1½ × 3½ × 11¼″ (peak stiffener)
S	2	1½ × 3½ × 11″ (railing)
T	2	¾ × 1½ × 20″ (slide cleat)
U	1	¾ × 20½ × 81″ plywood (slide)
V	4	¾ × 10 × 10″ plywood (gusset)
W1	1	½ × 40½ × 72″ plywood (roof)
W2	1	½ × 40 × 72″ plywood (roof)
X	4	½ × 3½ × 3½″ plywood (gusset)
Y	5	1″-dia. × 15″ wood dowels
Z	2½	Handsplit cedar shake bundles
AA		36″ × 18′ 15-lb. asphalt felt
BB	1	20 × 86″ rolled aluminum flashing
CC	1	Old tire
DD	1	⅜″-dia. × 9′ nylon rope
EE	36	⅜ × 4″ lagscrews and washers
FF	8	⅜ × 4″ capscrews, washers and nuts
GG	4	⅜ × 3½″ capscrews, washers and nuts
HH	2	⅜ × 5½″ capscrews, washers and nuts
II	4	⅜ × 4″ capscrews, washers and nuts
JJ	2	⅜ × 5½″ capscrews, washers and nuts
KK		2″ hot-dipped galvanized shake nails
LL		2″ hot-dipped galvanized roofing nails
MM		3″ hot-dipped galvanized nails
NN	8	6″ nails
OO		1¼″ hot-dipped galvanized nails

Misc.: Staples, waterproof glue, 6d and 4d common nails.

sharp. Begin by making the 35° angle cuts at the top of each post. Wear safety glasses and clamp the work firmly to your sawhorses. A chain saw does have muscle, and you don't want the posts shifting about during cutting.

Next, make the 35° shoulder cuts in the posts.

Then flop the post on its side and make the rip cut. By stopping both cuts just short of their mark, and removing the waste by hand, you will get the neatest possible joint. The straight notches are made in the outriggers with six parallel 1¾-in.-deep kerf cuts. Clean these out

THE OUTRIGGER is high enough to provide good sport, but low enough to be nonhazardous.

CLAMP POST firmly to sawhorse; keep saw level when making mitered shoulder cut.

STOP CUTS just short of desired depth. Finish the notch with a handsaw or chisel.

with a sharp chisel, keeping in mind that all edges will be exposed.

Cut all four rafters to length, then cut the tail detail with a sabre saw. Use waterproof glue and 2-in., hot-dipped galvanized nails to attach the plywood gussets to both sides. Because there are no joists or collar beams in this tower, it is extremely important that the joint between the rafters be properly constructed.

Next, working on a flat surface such as your garage floor or driveway, lay the posts down in pairs. After making certain that the paired posts are parallel and square to each other, tack-nail three braces between them, one each at the top, bottom and on the diagonal.

By setting the rafter assemblies into the shoulder cuts and clamping them in place, you can bore the holes for both simultaneously and thereby assure proper alignment. Bolt the rafter assemblies to each pair of posts as shown.

Cut the deck joists and base members next and assemble with lagscrews and washers.

Be sure that you bore pilot holes to prevent splitting. After the joists and deck members are complete, attach them to the four posts and nail

the ridge and roof supports between the rafters. Again, check for square and use braces between each pair of posts.

Now, dig four holes for the posts with a clamshell posthole digger. Make certain that the centers of the holes form a square with 44½-in. sides. The postholes should have a diameter of about 8 in. and be 28 in. deep. Pour 6 in. of gravel into each hole.

It is best to move the tower now, before it gets any heavier. Once you stand it in the holes, rock it slightly to seat it in the gravel. If the structure has remained square during the move, all that's needed is to plumb it and hold it that way with several diagonal braces secured to the posts on one end and to the stakes on the other end. Next, pour concrete around all posts.

Cut the roof panels from ½-in. plywood, as in the drawing, and attach them to the rafters and supports with 6d common nails. Because the underside is the visible surface, put the better side of

TO AVOID ERROR, use a felt pen to mark a clear line; the Xs show which side is waste.

HOLD SAW at downward angle and rip slowly. Taking extra time now will pay off later.

MAKE INSIDE notches 1¾-in. deep with repeated saw-kerf cuts spaced ⅜ in. apart.

USE A WIDE CHISEL to remove waste, straighten edges and level the bottom of the notch.

the panels down. Add the peak stiffeners (R) by nailing them from above with 4d common nails. Hold each stiffener securely with one hand while you drive the nails from above with the other.

Next, staple on 15-lb. felt to cover the roof, overlapping the peak. Then apply the hand-split cedar shakes using 4d, hot-dipped galvanized nails. These nails extend through the plywood and *must be clipped flush to the surface with an end nipper.*

The holes for the swing and the dowels can now be bored in the outriggers and the dowels glued in place. Then bolt the outriggers to the posts. Next, preassemble the railing units with nails and glue to assure maximum strength and notch them as shown to fit over the outrigger bolts that extend past the posts.

Bolt the railings to the posts and joists, then cut the lower railings below the outriggers. These are nailed in place from the far side of the post with 6-in. nails. Pilot holes should be bored first to

prevent splitting.

The slide is made by stapling 20-in.-wide aluminum flashing to the plywood along the edges; the heads will be covered later by the slide sides. Because aluminum flashing comes in a roll, it tends to curl, so cut it to length and reroll it in the opposite direction to straighten it out. At the top and bottom of the plywood, gently bend the flashing around the edge to avoid creasing and then nail the cleats over the ragged edges as shown.

Complete the slide by sanding all edges and making the slide support. Support holes have to be dug about 1 ft. deep for this. They can be positioned by merely holding the slide in its proper location and marking where the holes should be. No gravel or concrete is needed in these holes, but be sure to tamp down the backfilled dirt.

Finally, attach the slide and the ladder with capscrews as shown and cut and nail the deck boards to the joists.

Water hoop for summer fun

■ THIS ROLLICKING water hoop enables you to water the lawn at the same time the kids are having a ball jumping "rope" and getting drenched as the hoop turns. Strong jets of water escaping from pinholes drilled in opposite ends of the hoop cause the hoop to turn Ferris-wheel fashion when it's connected to a hose.

You can make one like it from ½-in. PVC pipe and standard plumbing fittings. The hoop turns on two supporting posts anchored in the ground, and a double female hose coupling prevents the garden hose from twisting into a pretzel as the hoop turns. PVC pipe tees, plus short pipe nipples, provide axles at the center point of the hoop. The hoop is easily assembled with regular PVC cement.

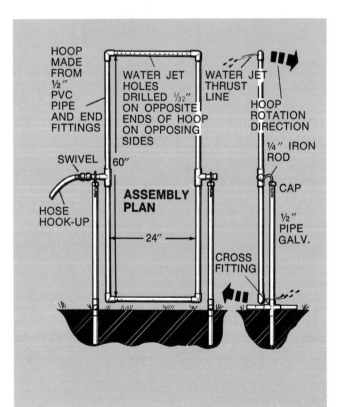

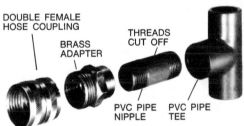

HOSE HOOKUP is assembled from standard brass fittings. Adapter threads take PVC nipple.

Jungle-gym tree house

■ A COMBINATION JUNGLE GYM and tree house such as this can be constructed very easily. The whole thing is designed to take advantage of standard lumber lengths and widths, which simplify construction. All you have to do is cut the various members to length.

The main platform is 6 ft. off the ground and supported by four 4 x 4 corner posts that are buried in 2 ft. of concrete. Each of the two levels measures 4 x 4 ft. square which means that both platforms can be cut from one 4 x 8-ft. sheet of ½-in. exterior-grade plywood. A 24-in. square hole is made in the lower platform for a fireman's pole. The pole is 1¼-in. galvanized pipe and is anchored at the top in a 2 x 4 crossrail and at the bottom in a hole filled with concrete. A seesaw uses the same pipe to pivot on. Two vertical ladders and a third one at approximately 60° are used here.

Designing different levels, ladders, poles and trapeze bars can be half the fun of construction. After all, your youngsters and their interests are different from all others!

Seesaw with a new twist

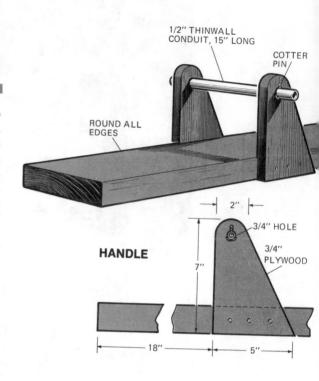

1/2" THINWALL CONDUIT, 15" LONG

COTTER PIN

ROUND ALL EDGES

HANDLE

2"

3/4" HOLE

3/4" PLYWOOD

7"

18"

5"

■ THIS SEESAW has a new twist and is sure to be irresistible to children of all ages. In addition to the usual up-and-down movement, the seat board rotates on a vertical shaft that's fitted with a thrust bearing. The shaft in turn fits inside a pipe post that's anchored and braced solidly to a nontipping base of 2 x 4s. For safety, you would be wise to rope off the area in which the seesaw rotates and provide only one entrance to eliminate any possibility of a child who's among the spectators getting bowled over and injured.

Use a sound 2 x 8 plank for the seat board and round all edges to prevent splinters. To finish the seesaw, apply two coats of exterior house paint. You'll probably want to use a lubricant on the moving parts to assure a quiet, trouble-free action. Notice that conduit clamps are used to attach the seat board to the steel rod that pivots in pipe-nipple bearings. A ⅜ x 5-in. carriage bolt is used to secure the seat board support to the 1-in. pipe used for the pivot.

YOUNGSTERS GET lots of exercise on this seesaw that takes them around as well as up and down.

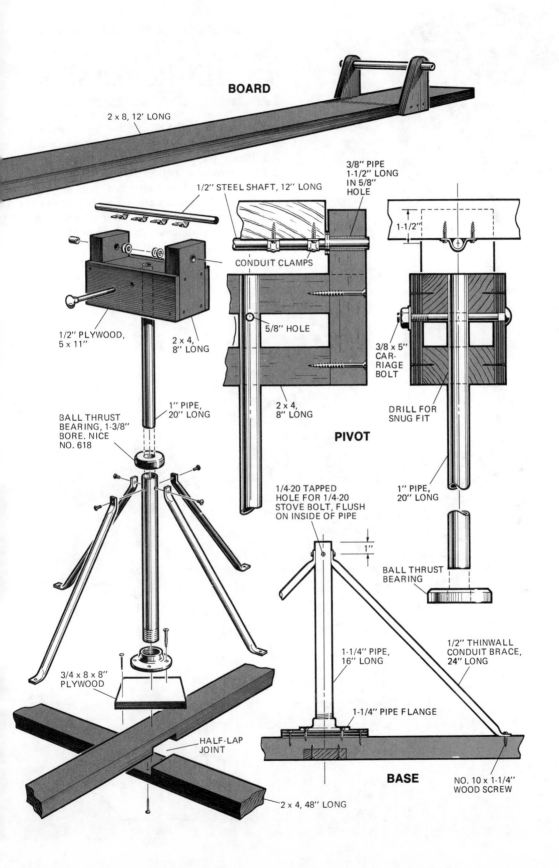

BOARD

2 x 8, 12' LONG

1/2" STEEL SHAFT, 12" LONG

3/8" PIPE 1-1/2" LONG IN 5/8" HOLE

CONDUIT CLAMPS

1-1/2"

1/2" PLYWOOD, 5 x 11"

2 x 4, 8" LONG

5/8" HOLE

3/8 x 5" CARRIAGE BOLT

BALL THRUST BEARING, 1-3/8" BORE. NICE NO. 618

1" PIPE, 20" LONG

2 x 4, 8" LONG

DRILL FOR SNUG FIT

PIVOT

1" PIPE, 20" LONG

1/4-20 TAPPED HOLE FOR 1/4-20 STOVE BOLT, FLUSH ON INSIDE OF PIPE

1"

BALL THRUST BEARING

3/4 x 8 x 8" PLYWOOD

1-1/4" PIPE, 16" LONG

1/2" THINWALL CONDUIT BRACE, 24" LONG

1-1/4" PIPE FLANGE

HALF-LAP JOINT

BASE

NO. 10 x 1-1/4" WOOD SCREW

2 x 4, 48" LONG

Stilt-house slide

■ YOUR CHILDREN will get your money's worth of fun and then some from this combined stilt house, playground slide and monkey bars. It's inexpensive to build, and remember, it's an item you'll be able to sell when your moppets outgrow it. Make it in sections and bolt them together for easy dismantling. Other than the pipe bars, you'll find all materials at your lumberyard. The drawings give you all the construction data you need. Set it on bricks so the legs don't sink in the ground. Coat the slide with a clear sealer and then paint the rest of the structure in bright colors.

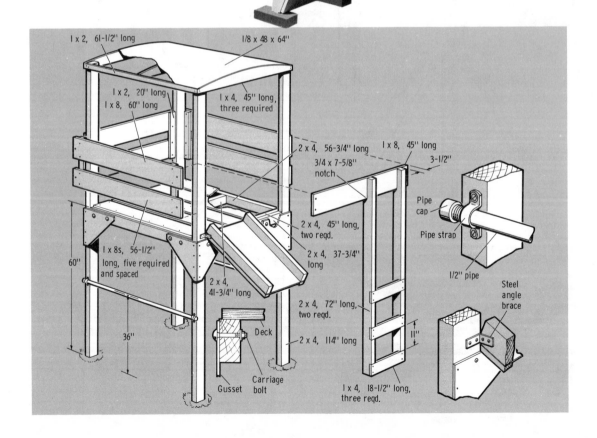

Playhouse you can build

■ WHETHER YOU NEED a playhouse for your youngsters, a summer office, pool cabana or more storage space for yard equipment, a lawn building like this is what you need.

Though the house can be built on a slab, it can also be constructed on four concrete-block piers. Evaluate exactly what you'll store in the shed,

then modify these plans to meet your space requirements.

Extra attention to details—window boxes, cupola birdhouse and ornamental hardware—gives the touches that elevate this little house from the construction-shanty look frequently found in home-built yard structures.

SHED FRAMING rests on four piers. Then flooring is nailed to joists and trimmed in place.

PLACE END WALLS and hold them temporarily with diagonal bracing. Ends equal the platform width.

SPEED CONSTRUCTION by assembling each wall on the ground, then hoisting it into place as a unit.

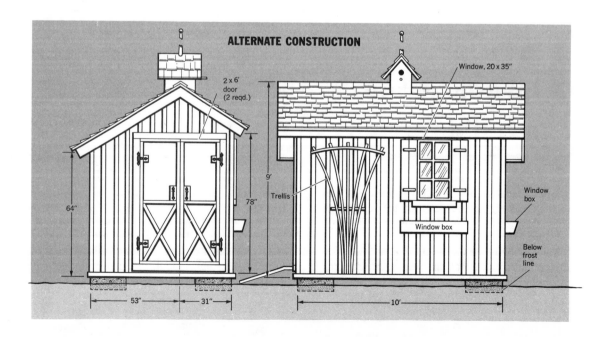

ALTERNATE CONSTRUCTION

2 x 6' door (2 reqd.)

Window, 20 x 35"

Trellis

Window box

Window box

Below frost line

9'

78"

64"

53"

31"

10'

ELEVATIONS

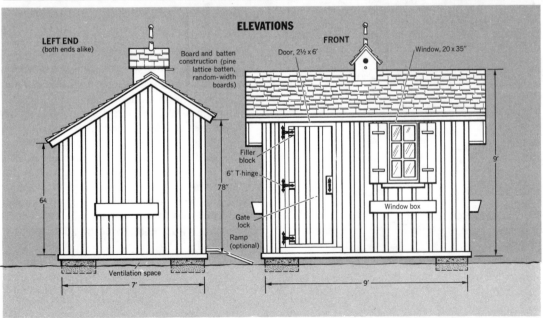

LEFT END
(both ends alike)

Board and batten
construction (pine
lattice batten,
random-width
boards)

FRONT

Door, 2½ x 6'

Window, 20 x 35"

Filler
block

6" T-hinge

Gate
lock

Ramp
(optional)

Ventilation space

Window box

64

78'

9'

7'

9'

Indoor playhouse

■ THIS QUICK-TO-SET-UP playhouse will delight your youngster. Walls can be ¼-in. plywood painted to suit or prefinished ¼-in. paneling. If the door opening is cut carefully, the cutout can become the door; window panes are also cut out, leaving muntins and bars. Furring strips for corner assembly and casing are glued and nailed; note that one longer corner strip serves to level walls held in end stands. Plywood strips lining door opening inside protrude ½ in. inward in order to keep the door from swinging in. Finishing touches are curtains and doorknobs, the latter made from thread spools.

MATERIALS for the playhouse are ¼-in. plywood for the walls, a sheet of paneling for the roof, furring strips and 2x4 scraps, beveled and slotted for the roof supports. The corner is held together with three ¼-in. bolts through the furring strips on both plywood walls.

48" LONG FURRING STRIP

18"

5"

15"

36"

48"

INNER DOOR LINING OF 3/8" PLYWOOD

DOOR CASING OF 1 x 2 FURRING STRIPS

18" 18"

1/4" HOLES, DRILL THREE

90"

CASING OF 1 x 2 FURRING STRIPS

12"

48"

24"

18"

WINDOW CENTERED ON END WALL

17"

2 x 4s NOTCHED TO HOOK OVER WALLS

1/4 x 24 x 96" ROOF PANEL. MAKE 2, ONE RIGHT, ONE LEFT

2 x 4 RAFTER 24" LONG 6 REQD.

8"

1/4 x 2" BOLT

45°

1/4" SLOT, 2-1/2" DEEP

1/4" SIDE WALL

1 x 2 x 12"

1/4" SLOT

12"

45°

1 x 2 x 24"

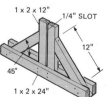

CUSTOMARY TO METRIC (CONVERSION) Conversion factors can be carried so far they become impractical. In cases below where an entry is exact it is followed by an asterisk (*). Where considerable rounding off has taken place, the entry is followed by a + or a − sign.

Linear Measure

inches	millimeters
1/16	1.5875*
1/8	3.2
3/16	4.8
1/4	6.35*
5/16	7.9
3/8	9.5
7/16	11.1
1/2	12.7*
9/16	14.3
5/8	15.9
11/16	17.5
3/4	19.05*
13/16	20.6
7/8	22.2
15/16	23.8
1	25.4*

inches	centimeters
1	2.54*
2	5.1
3	7.6
4	10.2
5	12.7*
6	15.2
7	17.8
8	20.3
9	22.9
10	25.4*
11	27.9
12	30.5

feet	centimeters	meters
1	30.48*	.3048*
2	61	.61
3	91	.91
4	122	1.22
5	152	1.52
6	183	1.83
7	213	2.13
8	244	2.44
9	274	2.74
10	305	3.05
50	1524*	15.24*
100	3048*	30.48*

1 yard = .9144* meters
1 rod = 5.0292* meters
1 mile = 1.6 kilometers
1 nautical mile = 1.852* kilometers

Weights

ounces	grams
1	28.3
2	56.7
3	85
4	113
5	142
6	170
7	198
8	227
9	255
10	283
11	312
12	340
13	369
14	397
15	425
16	454

Formula (exact):
ounces × 28.349 523 125* = grams

pounds	kilograms
1	.45
2	.9
3	1.4
4	1.8
5	2.3
6	2.7
7	3.2
8	3.6
9	4.1
10	4.5

1 short ton (2000 lbs) = 907 kilograms (kg)
Formula (exact):
pounds × .453 592 37* = kilograms

Fluid Measure

(Milliliters [ml] and cubic centimeters [cc] are equivalent, but it is customary to use milliliters for liquids.)

1 cu in = 16.39 ml
1 fl oz = 29.6 ml
1 cup = 237 ml
1 pint = 473 ml
1 quart = 946 ml
= .946 liters
1 gallon = 3785 ml
= 3.785 liters
Formula (exact):
fluid ounces × 29.573 529 562 5*
= milliliters

Volume

1 cu in = 16.39 cubic centimeters (cc)
1 cu ft = 28 316.7 cc
1 bushel = 35 239.1 cc
1 peck = 8 809.8 cc

Area

1 sq in = 6.45 sq cm
1 sq ft = 929 sq cm
= .093 sq meters
1 sq yd = .84 sq meters
1 acre = 4 046.9 sq meters
= .404 7 hectares
1 sq mile = 2 589 988 sq meters
= 259 hectares
= 2.589 9 sq kilometers

Miscellaneous

1 British thermal unit (Btu) (mean) = 1 055.9 joules
1 horsepower = 745.7 watts
= .75 kilowatts
caliber (diameter of a firearm's bore in hundredths of an inch) = .254 millimeters (mm)

1 atmosphere pressure = 101 325* pascals (newtons per sq meter)
1 pound per square inch (psi) = 6 895 pascals
1 pound per square foot = 47.9 pascals
1 knot = 1.85 kilometers per hour
1 mile per hour = 1.6093 kilometers per hour